LOST RECIPES

— OF THE —

AMERICAN REVOLUTION

56 Historic Recipes Inspired by 18th-Century America

A Culinary Exploration of the American Revolution from the Author of Lost Letters of the American Revolution

ELIZABETH WINSLOW

DEDICATION

"To all who gather at the table — may these receipts nourish not only your body, but also your sense of history. And to the dreamers and cooks who believe every recipe tells a story worth remembering."

TABLE OF CONTENTS

INTRODUCTION

In the years of America's birth, the kitchen was the beating heart of a new nation. Fires crackled in brick hearths, and heavy iron pots swung over glowing coals. Families gathered not only to eat, but to plan, to grieve, to celebrate, and to endure. These kitchens were places where news traveled faster than any postal rider—where the fate of the Revolution was whispered between women kneading bread, and where children learned that every crumb mattered.

Born of that same fire, this book invites you to step back into those kitchens. Within these pages are recipes once cooked, shared, and remembered during the American Revolution. More than a cookbook, it is a record of survival and of taste. Each recipe is paired with a story—drawn from archives, diaries, and family papers, or carefully reconstructed from contemporary accounts. Together, they carry voices across centuries: a widow stretching her flour in wartime, a tavern keeper serving cider punch to weary soldiers, a Loyalist exile writing home about the remembered taste of gooseberries in a foreign land. This collection of 56 historic recipes reflects the lives of the signers of the Declaration of Independence, honoring the everyday lives behind America's founding moment.

Some dishes were born of abundance—roast chicken with apple stuffing, plum pudding, and ginger cordial. Others rose from want corn cakes and root stews, reimagined here to please the modern table. The people of that time ate with ingenuity, turning scarcity into flavor, hardship into hospitality.

Each recipe holds the weight of a moment in history, a single thread in the larger tapestry of how America was fed—in body and in spirit—during its most fragile years. In preserving them, this book becomes more than instruction; it becomes remembrance.

Figure 1. Colonial cooking utensils. AI-generated artwork, 2025.

BASIC COLONIAL COOKING UTENSILS

- **Dutch Ovens** – Heavy cast-iron pots with flat lids to hold coals for baking breads, pies, and roasts.

- **Spits and Racks** – For roasting meat in front of the fire; turned by hand or, in wealthier homes, by a mechanical spit-jack.

- **Bake Kettles** – Smaller versions of Dutch ovens, often used for cornbread or puddings.

- **Long-handled Utensils** – Skimmers, ladles, and forks with extra-long handles to keep the cook's hands (and skirts) away from the flames.

- **Porringers** – Small bowls with handles for serving porridges, stews, and pottages.

- **Butter Churns** – Dash or barrel types for turning cream into butter.

- **Mortar and Pestle** – For grinding spices, herbs, and grains.

COLONIAL KITCHEN CONVERSION

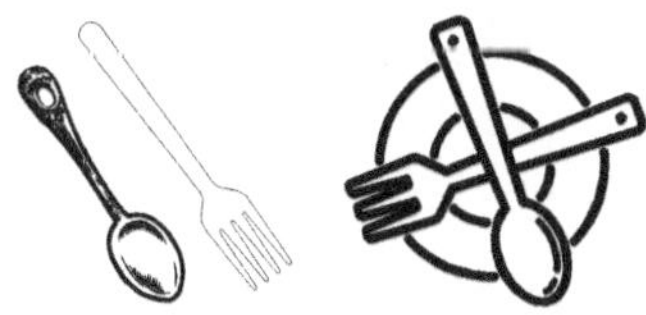

Colonial Kitchen
Conversion Chart

DRY MEASURES

Salt Spoon ⅓ tsp

1 Tea spoon 1 tsp

1 Dessert spoon = 2 tsp

1 Table spoon = 3 tsp

1 Gill 5 oz

4 Noggin 2 cups

4 Bushel 4 pecks

OVEN HEAT

Slow Oven 250 – 300° F+

Moderate Oven 375-400°F

Quick Oven 425°F+

Hot Oven 425°F+

LIQUID MEASURES

1 Wine glass ¼ cup

1 Tea cup ¾ cup

1 Coffee cup 6 oz

1 Gill ½ cup

2 Quart 4 cups

WEIGHT

1 Dram 1/16 oz

1 Ounce 28 g

1 Pound 16 oz

ABBREVIATIONS

TSP- TEASPOON   LB- POUND
TBSP- TABLESPOON DOZ- DOZEN
PT- PINT
OZ- OUNCES

Figure 2. Colonial Kitchen Conversion Chart. AI-generated artwork, 2025.

A NOTE TO THE READER

As you read the stories that accompany these receipts—some written in ink on yellowed letters, others passed hand to hand—imagine the lives behind them. They reflect a world in which cooking was guided less by exact measurements and temperatures than by experience, judgment, and the rhythms of daily life. For each dish, you will find two distinct parts. The **Original Receipt** appears as it was written or closely paraphrased from period sources. These receipts preserve the language, assumptions, and style of early cooks, who expected the reader to understand terms such as 'moderate oven,' 'quick oven,' and 'bake gently,' and who measured by handfuls, spoonfuls, and instinct rather than precision.

The **Modern Recipe** follows, translating those historical instructions into a form suitable for a contemporary kitchen. Measurements are clarified, cooking times are suggested, and modern equipment is assumed—while the spirit, ingredients, and intent of the original are carefully preserved.

You may notice that some directions allow for flexibility, and this is intentional. Eighteenth-century cooking depended on variables we no longer share: hearth fires instead of thermostats, seasonal ingredients, and kitchens shaped by circumstance rather than standardization. To cook historically is to observe, adjust, and respond. These recipes invite you to do the same.

Throughout the book, period cooking language is retained wherever possible. Historical terms are frequently found in eighteenth-century receipts. The modern equivalents provided are intended as guides rather than rigid rules.

INTERPRETING HISTORICAL COOKING TERMS

Historical Term	Suggested Modern Cue
Moderate Oven	350-375F°
Quick Oven	400-425F°
Slow Oven	300-325F°
Bake Gently	Lower end of stated range
Before a Brisk Fire	Medium-high heat

These ranges are meant to orient the modern cook while preserving the flexibility that was central to historical practice. Trust your senses as much as your tools.

Finally, you will find blank pages set aside for your own notes. Early cooks routinely annotated their books—crossing out lines, adding remarks, and adapting receipts to their households. In that tradition, you are encouraged to record what works best in your kitchen, the changes you make, and the memories these dishes create.

This book is not meant to be read once and set aside. It is meant to be used, marked, and returned to—much as the originals were.

COLONIAL BREADS

Bread was the daily anchor of the colonial diet. No meal felt complete without it. In humble cabins and grand houses alike, loaves and cakes of grain defined the table. During the Revolution, bread was more than sustenance—it was survival, identity, and, at times, a symbol of politics.

For most households, cornbread and rye bread were the staples of everyday life. Wheat, though prized, was costly and often scarce in New England, where thin soils made it challenging to grow. Cornmeal, by contrast, was plentiful. Families baked it into hearty loaves, ash cakes cooked on the hearth, or "Johnnycakes" fried on griddles. Rye was often mixed with corn or wheat to make dense, dark loaves that kept well and filled hungry stomachs.

In regions where wheat was more abundant—the Mid-Atlantic and the Southern colonies—families baked lighter breads and rolls. Wealthier households enjoyed fine white loaves, made from imported or estate-grown flour, while poorer families relied on coarse brown bread. The Revolution sharpened these contrasts. Patriot leaders urged Americans to embrace corn and rye as symbols of independence, turning away from the refined British wheat they had once prized.

Bread was also the food of travel and the soldier's constant companion. Hardtack—a simple biscuit of flour and water, baked until nearly indestructible—sustained both armies and sailors. Tough to chew but slow to spoil, it made endurance possible. In towns and taverns, bread was always present: paired with cheese, dipped in broth, or served with butter, honey, or molasses when fortune allowed.

Colonial bread recipes were guidelines, not guarantees. Measurements were approximate, ovens unpredictable, and ingredients ever changing. Cooks learned to judge dough by touch and smell, not by teaspoons. The result was bread that reflected circumstance as much as skill—shaped by season, scarcity, and necessity. In recreating these breads today, we step into that same tradition of adaptation.

FRENCH ROLLS

In the young kitchens of the early republic, when the hearth was the nucleus of daily life, the smell of rising bread could awaken an entire household. Among the humbler loaves—hoecakes, fire cakes, journey bread—there was a touch of elegance reserved for Sundays, for company, or for a long-awaited visit from distant kin: the French roll.

Amelia Simmons, the first American-born cookbook author, gifted her readers this gently luxurious bread in her 1796 landmark work, *American Cookery*. In an age when yeast was scarce and ovens uncertain, these rolls demanded both care and patience. Simmons's instructions, written without exact weights or measures, called for a quart of warmed milk, a bit of butter, and a spoonful or two of yeast. The dough was to be "light," pliant under the hand, shaped into small rounds, and baked to a golden hue.

The French roll bridged two worlds—evoking Old World refinement in a New World kitchen. It was not an everyday bread. It required time, attention, and ingredients not easily found on the frontier. But to pull a pan of them from the embers or an iron oven, browned and steaming, was to offer more than food. It was to show skill and patience, to extend hospitality and gentility, and to affirm a connection to a wider world. These were the dinner rolls of those who dreamed beyond the horizon.

<u>Original Receipt</u>

To make light French rolls. Take a quart of milk warmed, a quarter of a pound of butter, and two spoons of good yeast. Mix in flour sufficiently to make a light dough. Work it well, let it rise, and when it is risen, form into small rolls. Let them rise again and bake in a moderate oven until light brown.

<u>Modern Recipe</u>

Skill Level: Easy
Prep Time: 20 minutes
Cook Time: 18-22 minutes
Total Time: 2 - 2½ hours, including rising
Yield: 8 – 10 rolls

FRENCH ROLLS (Continued)

Ingredients

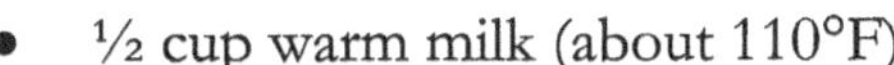

- 2 cups of bread flour

- ½ cup warm milk (about 110°F)

- ¼ cup warm water

- 1 tbsp sugar

- 2 tsp active dry yeast

- ½ tsp salt

- 2 tbsp butter, softened

Directions

1. In a small bowl, mix warm water, milk, and sugar. Sprinkle the yeast over and let it sit until it becomes foamy (5–10 minutes).

2. In a large bowl, combine flour and salt. Add yeast mixture and butter. Mix until the dough forms.

3. Knead on a floured surface 8–10 min, until smooth and elastic.

4. Place the dough in a greased bowl, cover, and let it rise for 1 hour. Or until doubled in size.

5. Punch down the dough and divide into 8–10 equal pieces. Shape into rounds.

6. Place on parchment-lined baking sheet. Cover and let rise for an additional 30–45 minutes.

7. Preheat oven to 375°F and bake 18–22 min.

8. Serve warm, with butter.

HOECAKES

At Mount Vernon, George Washington began each morning not with speeches or strategy, but with silence—and with hoecakes swimming in butter and honey. These small cakes of cornmeal, crisped on a griddle and drenched in sweetness, were neither a soldier's ration nor a statesman's indulgence. They were a ritual of comfort, repeated morning after morning, long before sunrise. His step-granddaughter, Eleanor "Nelly" Parke Custis Lewis, would later recall that the General always took his hoecakes with tea—served in modest portions, but with unwavering routine.

These hoecakes were leavened by patience: a batter left to rest overnight, raised by yeast and the warmth of a quiet kitchen. Each spoonful was dropped onto a hot iron surface and fried in butter or suet until golden at the edges. The honey was local, the butter likely churned nearby.

Though Washington's days were burdened with revolution, politics, and the mythmaking of a nation coming into being, his breakfast remained humble—Southern, familiar, and steadfast. It reminded him, perhaps, that the man who led armies and presided over constitutions was still rooted in the same sweet taste of home.

For a man with fragile teeth and an iron will, these hoecakes were more than sustenance. They were solace and ceremony—a private moment of constancy amid the clamor of public life. In an age of powdered wigs and powdered muskets, there is something beautifully human in knowing that George Washington, every single day, liked his breakfast hot and honeyed.

Original Receipt

Take one pint of Indian meal, and half a teaspoon of salt. Pour over one pint of boiling water and stir well to form a thick batter. Let it stand to settle. When the fire is hot, and the griddle clean and grease, drop the batter by spoonful upon the iron. Fry in fresh butter until browned upon both sides. Serve warm, with honey or molasses.

HOECAKES (Continued)

<u>Modern Recipe</u>

Skill Level: Easy
Prep Time: 10 minutes
Cook Time: 10-15 minutes
Total Time: 25 minutes
Yield: 6-8 Hoecakes

Ingredients

- 1 cup of cornmeal (fine ground)
- ½ tsp salt
- 1 cup of boiling water
- 2 tbsp of unsalted butter (plus more for frying)
- Honey, for serving

Directions

1. In a bowl, mix the cornmeal and salt.
2. Carefully pour the boiling water over the cornmeal mixture, stirring until smooth. Let it sit for 5–10 minutes to thicken slightly.
3. Heat a skillet or griddle over medium heat and add a small amount of butter.
4. Drop batter by heaping tablespoon onto the skillet, forming small cakes (about 3 inches wide).
5. Fry 2 – 3 minutes per side, or until golden brown and crisp on the edges.
6. Serve hot, drenched in melted butter and honey, as Washington preferred.

Historical Note: *Washington had a sweet tooth: By the end of his life, Washington had only one natural tooth left. But every morning, he still insisted on hoecakes—sweet, warm, and familiar.*

LIBERTY BREAD

This letter from Hannah Brewer, a Boston housewife writing in 1774, offers a glimpse into the domestic front lines of the American Revolution. The bread she describes— "Liberty Bread"—was a mixture of rye flour and Indian cornmeal, born of necessity and sharpened into protest. As colonial women boycotted British wheat, they turned to native grains, transforming every loaf into a quiet act of defiance.

Hannah's tone is affectionate yet unyielding, her household labor transfigured into rebellion. When she writes of "beating the dough with fury," as if striking a Redcoat, the image carries both humor and conviction. Her kitchen becomes a battleground, her bread a symbol— sustenance mingled with principle, the ordinary made revolutionary.

Boston, the 9th Day of October 1774

My Dearest Samuel,

The oven was lit before dawn, and the house filled with the sour-sweet scent of rye and meal. I have again taken to baking our Liberty Bread—the Rye and Indian as the women now call it in jest, though our purpose is far from jesting. We will have no more of British wheat, not while our men sit in Congress to speak our cause. I stirred the cornmeal with my own hand and thought of you with every sweep of the spoon. The dough was stubborn, but I beat it with all the fury I might give to a Redcoat.

It is coarse bread, to be sure. It bears the grit of the earth and the bitter edge of molasses, but it fills the belly and steels the will. I laid the loaves upon the hearthstone and watched them rise, not as soft English rolls, but firm, resolute— American.

Mrs. Alcott says her husband mocks the stuff, calls it cattle feed. Let him eat his pride when the wheat ships stop. The children miss the sweet rolls, but I tell them this is Patriot Bread, and they take it with solemn mouths. The boy Thomas asked the King if he ate such bread. I told him no, and he spat his bite into the fire. I send two loaves wrapped in linen. Share them with Mr. Adams or that tall Virginian whose name I forget. Tell them it was made with Boston hands, and Boston resolve. Write me when you can. The weather turns and I worry for your health. We are strong here. We knead our cause into every crust.

LIBERTY BREAD (Continued)

Your devoted wife,

Hannah

Original Receipt

Mix rye and cornmeal well. Pour boiling milk over the mix; stir vigorously. Let it cool until lukewarm, then add yeast. Knead into a stiff dough; let it rise in a warm place until it cracks on top. Shape into two loaves and bake in a moderate oven for 2½ hours.

Modern Recipe

Skill Level: Moderate

Prep Time: 25 minutes

Cook Time: 50 -55 minutes

Total Time: 2½ -3 hours (including rising)

Yield: 1 loaf

Ingredients

- 1¼ cups cornmeal
- 2 cups of rye and strong whole wheat flour
- 1 tsp salt
- 1 tbsp molasses (or black treacle)
- 1 tbsp butter
- ¾ cup and 1 tbsp water
- ⅓ cup beer
- 1 tsp dried yeast

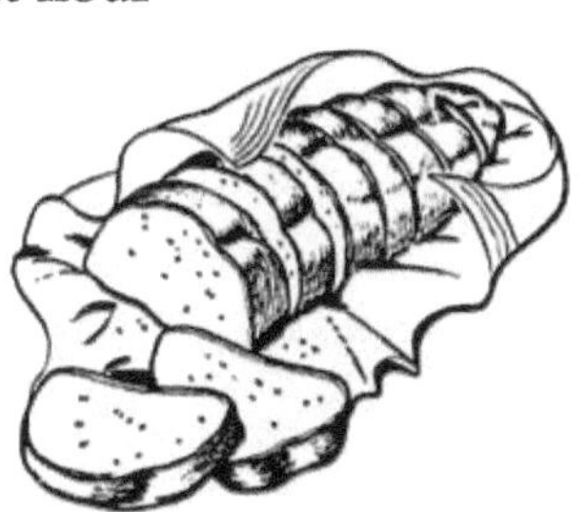

Directions

1. Combine dry ingredients.
2. Melt butter and molasses; mix with water and beer.

3. Combine and knead for ~10 min.

4. Rise for one hour, shape the loaf, and then rise for 45 minutes.

5. Bake: 400°F (15 min), then reduce the heat to 350°F and bake for 35 – 40 minutes.

SALLY LUNN BREAD

While ragged soldiers at Valley Forge gnawed on fire cakes—crude patties of flour and water baked on hot stones until they were more ash than bread—the dining tables of Williamsburg told another story. In taverns lit by candlelight, and in the parlors of Virginia's elite, Sally Lunn was served warm and golden, its rich crumb heavy with butter, eggs, and milk.

Picture a young officer, weary of drills, slipping into the Raleigh Tavern. He finds warmth, laughter, and the soft comfort of Sally Lunn—a bread that tastes of home, of civility, of a world worth fighting for. In Martha Washington's own recipe book, the bread appears, a reminder that even in wartime, refinement and hospitality endure.

Sally Lunn bridged two worlds: the rough-hewn colonies and the polished manners of England. To eat it was to believe that hardship might one day yield to gentility. It was a bread of hope as much as of flavor—whispering that liberty would not always taste of ash and hunger.

Original Receipt

Take a quart of warmed milk, a quarter of a pound of butter, six eggs well beaten, a spoonful of sugar, and a gill of good yeast. Stir in flour enough to make a thick batter. Beat it well, set it to rise before the fire, and when light, bake it in a moderate oven.

Modern Recipe

Skill Level: Moderate
Prep Time: 25 minutes
Cook Time: 50 - 55 minutes
Total Time: 2½ - 3 hours including rising
Yield: 1 loaf

Ingredients

- 1 cup milk

- ½ cup shortening

SALLY LUNN BREAD (Continued)

- ¼ cup water

- 4 cups sifted all-purpose flour (divided)

- ⅓ cup of sugar

- 1 teaspoon of salt

- 2 packages of active dry yeast

- 3 eggs

Directions

1. Grease a 10-inch cake pan.

2. Heat milk, shortening, and ¼ cup water until warm, not hot.

3. In a large bowl, blend ⅓ cup of flour with sugar, salt, and dry yeast.

4. Stir in the warm milk mixture until blended.

5. Add enough of the remaining flour (about 3 more cups) to make a thick, smooth batter. It should not form a stiff dough.

6. Cover and let rise for about 30- 45 minutes.

7. Spoon into the greased pan, cover again, and let rise until it nearly doubled.

8. Bake: 350°F (1 hour). Sally Lunn is delicious sliced when cold, buttered, and toasted.

WIDOW'S BREAD

In the letter titled *Widow's Bread*, Hannah Peters measures her grief in pounds of flour and pinches of salt. Her husband, John, has died at the Battle of Camden—an August 1780 disaster for the Continental Army in South Carolina. But news traveled slowly, and by the time word reached Hannah in Massachusetts, it came not by official notice or solemn dispatch, but through a neighbor repeating a rumor. This form of communication was how many Revolutionary widows learned of loss: no ceremony, no body to bury, only silence broken by whispers.

Yet Hannah found ritual in her baking. She wrote to her sister:

Dear Sister Sarah, I write to you with hands still dusted white—not from the softness of new snow, but from the coarse meal I've just beat into a passable dough. The bread will not rise as it used to. It sits heavy in the pan, like the sorrow in my chest. It has been near three months since John fell at Camden. The news came slow, wrapped in the halting pity of our neighbor, who had it from a militiaman just returned. I did not weep when I heard it. I set down my needle, stirred the fire, and made bread. What else is there to do? Flour is now twenty-two shillings the stone, and salt dearer still. I bartered two combs and a spoon for a half-sack from Mr. Harlan, who had it hid in his loft. He said the British blockade has choked the ports; what little we have comes dear. Yet still I bake—for the boys, for the memory of John, who loved the heel crust best.

— Your Sister, Hannah

Original Receipt

- 2 pounds coarse-ground wheat flour

- 1 pound rye or cornmeal

- 1 tablespoon salt

- Warm water as needed

- Barm or sour leaven (if available)

Directions: "Mix flour and salt in a large bowl. Add warm water gradually to form stiff dough. Knead firmly; add leaven if on hand. Cover loosely; let rise near the hearth. Shape into dense loaves. Bake in a Dutch oven or brick hearth oven. Cool on a wooden board. Keep well for travel."

WIDOW'S BREAD (Continued)

Modern Recipe

Skill Level: Easy
Prep Time: 15 minutes
Cook Time: 10-20 minutes
Total Time: 45 minutes
Yield: 8 small rolls

Ingredients

- 2 cups of Flour (1 cup Whole Wheat + 1 cup White)

- 2 tablespoons of butter (softened)

- 1 tablespoon honey or molasses

- 1 teaspoon salt

- 2½ tsp active dry yeast (1 packet)

- ¾ cup warm water or warm milk

- 3 eggs

Directions

1. Mix dry ingredients.

2. Work butter with your fingertips

3. Add warm water, milk, and honey.

4. Knead gently for 3 minutes until smooth.

5. Rest the dough for 10–20 minutes.

6. Shape into small round rolls.

9. Bake: 350°F for 25–28 minutes, until lightly golden.

10. Brush with melted butter, then drizzle with honey while warm.

VEGETABLES

VEGETABLES

Vegetables were the quiet backbone of the colonial diet. While meat and bread often took center stage, it was the garden that sustained daily life. In a world before markets and stores, every family depended on what they could grow, preserve, or barter for—the yield of their own labor and the generosity of their neighbors.

The staples were humble and enduring. Cabbage, onions, turnips, carrots, and potatoes found their way into stews and soups through every season. Corn—the most American of crops—was eaten fresh in summer, or dried and ground into meal for bread and mush. In New England, beans joined corn in the beloved "succotash," a dish first taught by Native peoples. Pumpkins and squash appeared everywhere: baked, boiled, mashed, or even sliced and fried. Housewives filled their cellars with gourds and roots to see their families through the winter months.

Preservation was a daily art. Families pickled cucumbers, fermented cabbage into sauerkraut, and dried beans, apples, and corn—provisions that kept the table supplied when the fields lay bare. Broths were thickened with peas; pies filled with squash or pumpkin when apples ran short; and tender greens—dandelion, spinach, and others—were gathered from meadows and kitchen yards.

During the Revolution, vegetables came to stand for endurance itself. Whether boiled into stews for soldiers, baked into pies in taverns, or simmered in the hearths of family homes, they nourished both body and resolve when luxuries were gone. If roasts and sweets marked celebration, it was the steady rhythm of vegetables—from bean fields, corn patches, and garden plots—that truly fed the Revolution.

COLONIAL CORN AND BEAN POTTAGE

According to Oneida oral tradition, the winter of 1777–78 at Valley Forge was not merely cold—it was an abyss of suffering. The men of the Continental Army, ragged and sick, stood on the brink of collapse. With temperatures plunging to six degrees, boots worn to shreds, and coats reduced to rags, soldiers huddled together in cabins that could scarcely hold back the wind. Their stomachs were empty, their spirits, nearly so.

Then, from more than two hundred fifty miles away, came Polly Cooper—an Oneida woman who traveled with forty-seven Oneida warriors, carrying bushels of white corn. It was not the corn of Virginia or Connecticut, but of her people: carefully prepared, and preserved by traditional means. It was a gift of food, but also of knowledge, and of care.

Polly taught the soldiers how to soak, rinse, and slow-cook the kernels—how to turn them into a sustaining soup. When she could, she added nuts, dried fruit, and bone broth. And when the corn was gone, she stayed. She cooked, nursed, and listened, tending to the sick without any promise of reward. When the worst had passed, and the snow began to melt into the muddy beginnings of spring, she refused compensation. "It was my duty," she said, according to the Oneida.

In gratitude, Martha Washington presented Polly with a black shawl and bonnet—not mere tokens, but symbols of dignity and alliance. The Oneida Indian Nation preserves that shawl to this day, a testament to the friendship that helped sustain a fledgling country. Polly Cooper's journey remains one of the most humane and unheralded acts of the American Revolution.

Original Receipt

Soak dried corn and beans overnight. Simmer them in water or light broth, adding such vegetables as are at hand—onion, turnip, or parsnip—and a small piece of salted port or fat. Season with salt and cook until tender, according to the time specified.

COLONIAL CORN AND BEAN POTTAGE (Continued)

<u>Modern Recipe</u>

Skill Level: Moderate
Prep Time: 20 minutes
Cook Time: 45 minutes
Total Time: 1 hour 5 minutes
Yield: Serves 4 - 6

Ingredients

- 1 cup hominy (dried or canned)
- 1 cup canned white, navy, or cannellini beans
- 1 medium onion, diced
- 1 parsnip or turnip, peeled and diced
- 2 carrots, peeled and diced
- 2 cloves garlic, minced
- 1 tbsp olive oil or butter
- 4 cups of vegetables or chicken broth
- ½ cup diced smoked turkey or ham hock
- 1 bay leaf
- Salt and pepper, to taste

Directions

1. If using dried hominy, simmer it in water until tender (approximately 1 hour). Drain.

2. In a large pot, heat olive oil over medium. Add onion, carrots, parsnip/turnip, and garlic. Sauté 5–7 minutes until softened.

3. Stir in hominy and white beans. Add broth and bay leaf.

4. If using smoked turkey, add it now. If you use tempeh, wait until the last 10 minutes of simmering. Simmer gently for 30–40 minutes. Season with salt and pepper and serve with hot, crusty bread.

PUMPKIN WITH HERBS (STEWED PUMPKIN)

She was called the Conscience of the American Revolution. Mercy Otis Warren of Plymouth, Massachusetts, was no ordinary housewife. Sister to patriot James Otis, confidante of John Adams, and friend to Samuel and Abigail Adams, she wielded her pen as fiercely as any soldier bore a musket. From her study flowed biting satires, plays, and histories that mocked the power of the British Crown and gave eloquent voice to the cause of liberty.

Yet even as she helped shape a nation with her words, she tended the same domestic rhythms as any colonial woman. In her kitchen garden pumpkins, beans, and herbs, the humble staples of New England life grew. Around her table, patriots gathered not for banquets, but for simple stews seasoned with thyme and sage.

Pumpkin was no fleeting autumn indulgence, but a year-round companion in the colonial kitchen. Fresh from the garden in fall, it could be sliced and dried into leathery strips for winter, simmered in porridge, baked into bread, or mashed with herbs into savory stews. Even the seeds, roasted and salted, found their place by the hearth. For Mercy, this sturdy fruit was more than food; it was resilience served warm—sustenance for both household and revolution.

As she sharpened her satire into a weapon against tyranny, the scent of pumpkin and herbs rose from her hearth—a quiet reminder that independence was forged not only in battles and debates, but in kitchens and gardens, by women whose hands fed the cause of liberty.

Original Receipt

Take the pumpkin and pare it, and stew it till soft; strain it through a sieve, and put it into a pan, and let it dry away; put it in sweet milk and stew it gently; add a little sugar, ginger, and allspice.

Modern Recipe

Skill Level: Easy
Prep Time: 15 minutes
Cook Time: 25 - 30 minutes
Total Time: 40 – 45 minutes

PUMPKIN WITH HERBS (STEWED PUMPKIN) Continued

Yield: Serves 4

Ingredients

- 2 pounds pumpkin, peeled and cubed
- 2 tbsp butter (or olive oil)
- 1 tsp fresh thyme
- 1 tsp chopped fresh sage
- ½ tsp nutmeg
- Salt and pepper to taste

Directions

1. Roast pumpkin cubes at 400°F until tender and caramelized (20–25 min).
2. In a skillet, melt butter and sauté herbs until fragrant. Toss roasted pumpkin into herb butter. Add nutmeg, salt, and pepper.
3. Serve warm.

Pumpkin Beyond the Plate

Natural Potpourri

Colonists sometimes dried pumpkin rinds and seeds, then tucked them into sachets with herbs like rosemary, lavender, or mint to freshen trunks and cupboards. The earthy scent mingled with garden herbs to keep linens smelling sweet.

Seed Charms

Pumpkin seeds were strung as simple garlands, either to dry them for planting or to hang in kitchens as a reminder of the next year's crop.

Feed for Animals

Leftover pumpkin rinds and mash went to pigs, chickens, and cattle, ensuring nothing was lost.

Colonial pumpkins were used for:

- Bread and puddings 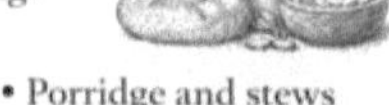
- Porridge and stews
- Small beer and animal feed 
- Preserves and storage 

MOLLY PITCHER'S SKILLET POTATOES

They knew her first as a wife, a washerwoman, a camp follower—one of the countless women who trailed the Continental Army, children on their hips and kettles on their backs. But at the Battle of Monmouth, in the blistering heat of June 1778, Mary Ludwig Hays became something more.

Again and again, she hauled water to the front lines as musket fire cracked and cannon smoke filled the air. To the parched soldiers, she was salvation itself, shouting her arrival as she brought a pitcher of water through the chaos. When her husband collapsed at his post beside the artillery, Mary stepped forward, took his place, and kept firing until the battle was won. The men called her Molly Pitcher.

Yet long before that single day of glory, Mary had been fighting a quieter war. In muddy camps, she boiled stews from roots scavenged or supplied—potatoes, onions, carrots—frying them in drippings over open fires. It was food born of necessity, stretched to feed many, but rich with the taste of survival.

Mary's story reminds us that women's work was never only domestic, never merely background. At the hearth or at the cannon's mouth, she embodied the Revolution's endurance. Her campfire hash, browned crisp in a skillet, may have seemed ordinary. But in the hunger of war, even the simplest dish could mean the difference between despair and strength.

She did not write treatises or sign declarations. Mary Ludwig Hays left her mark on history with sweat, smoke, and the ring of iron. And through her, we remember the thousands of women whose labor—both at the fire and under fire—helped bring a nation into being.

Original Receipt

Slice carrots, parsnips, or potatoes thin, fry them in dripping, with onions if you have them, till they be brown and crisp.

MOLLY PITCHER'S SKILLET POTATOES (Continued)

<u>Modern Recipe</u>

Skill Level: Easy
Prep Time: 10 minutes
Cook Time: 15-20 minutes
Total Time: 25 – 30 minutes
Yield: Serves 2 - 3

Ingredients

- 3 medium potatoes, diced

- 2 carrots, diced

- 1 large onion, diced

- 2 tbsp butter, lard, or drippings

- 1 tsp fresh thyme (or ½ tsp dried)

- Salt and pepper to taste

Directions

1. Heat butter or drippings in a large skillet over medium heat.

2. Add potatoes, carrots, and onion. Cook, stirring occasionally, until vegetables are browned and crisp (15–20 minutes).

3. Season with thyme, salt, and pepper.

4. Serve hot, straight from the pan.

SAUTÉED SUCCOTASH (CORN, BEANS, AND SQUASH)

She was kidnapped from Africa as a child and enslaved in Boston. Yet by the age of eighteen, Phillis Wheatley had become the first African American woman to publish a book of poetry in the colonies. Her verses spoke of liberty and faith at a time when her own life remained bound in chains.

In the Wheatley household, Phillis almost certainly ate from the kitchen garden that grew beans, corn, and squash—the "Three Sisters" cultivated by Native peoples long before Europeans arrived. These foods crossed boundaries of race and class, sustaining the enslaved and the free alike.

Succotash—a simple blend of corn, beans, and squash—was more than a dish. It was sustenance, survival, and remembrance on a single plate. In lean seasons, it was a meager ration; in times of plenty, a celebration of the harvest. For Phillis, who endured bondage yet wrote with transcendent grace, such a meal would have been deeply familiar nourishing her body even as her words nourished a vision of freedom far greater than herself.

Proceed, great chief, with virtue on thy side, Thy ev'ry action let the goddess guide.

— Phillis Wheatley, *Ode to George Washington*, 1776

Just as Phillis's verses sustained the spirit of liberty, humble foods like succotash sustained the body. Together, they nourished a Revolution.

SAUTEÉD SUCCOTASH (CORN, BEANS, AND SQUASH)
Continued

<u>Original Receipt</u>

From Amelia Simmons, *American Cookery* (Hartford, 1796):

Boil Indian corn till soft, add beans and garden roots, season with butter or salt.

<u>Modern Recipe</u>

Skill Level: Easy
Prep Time: 10 minutes
Cook Time: 15 minutes
Total Time: 25 minutes
Yield: Serves 4

Ingredients

- 2 cups of fresh or frozen corn kernels
- 1 cup lima beans (or green beans)
- 1 cup diced yellow squash or zucchini
- 2 tbsp butter (or olive oil)
- 1 tbsp fresh basil or parsley
- Salt and pepper to taste

Directions

1. Cook the beans until tender, then drain them.
2. In a skillet, melt butter.
3. Add corn and squash to the skillet.
4. Cook 5–7 minutes, stirring occasionally, until tender.
5. Stir in beans and season with salt, pepper, and fresh herbs.

GREEN BEANS WITH ALMONDS AND BUTTERED CABBAGE

Philadelphia's narrow streets once bustled with markets alive in color and scent. Housewives and artisans carried baskets on their arms, choosing from heaps of beans, cabbages, carrots, and potatoes while merchants called out their wares. The rhythm of that daily trade nourished not only bodies but the very cause of independence.

Betsy Ross lived here—not in a grand estate, but in a modest home and workshop, her hands were perpetually busy with needle and thread. The legend of her flag has come to define her, yet her life was stitched just as firmly into the fabric of the city itself. We have no record of her recipes, no journal of her suppers. But we know what filled the markets she frequented. French beans—what we now call green beans—were boiled until tender, then tossed with butter, salt, and pepper. Cabbage, another staple, was stewed in broth with butter and spice, filling kitchens with a scent both humble and sustaining.

Around Betsy's table, the meals were not lavish, but they carried the quiet dignity of care. Buttered beans, stewed cabbages simple fare for a city daring to dream of liberty. Betsy's world was one of work, of struggle, of patient perseverance. And just as her hands stitched the colors of a new nation, her city's markets stitched together the daily bread of revolution: green beans, cabbage, and the promise of something enduring.

Original Receipt

To Dress French Beans – *Boil your beans tender, but not too much; put them into a stew-pan with a little butter, salt, and pepper, and toss them up.*

To Stew Cabbage – *Take a cabbage, half-boil it, squeeze it dry, cut it small, put it into a stew-pan with broth, a little butter, pepper, and salt, stew it gently.*

Modern Recipes

GREEN BEANS WITH ALMONDS

Skill Level: Easy
Prep Time: 10 minutes
Cook Time: 5 - 7 minutes
Total Time: 15 – 20 minutes

GREEN BEANS WITH ALMONDS (Continued)

Yield: Serves 4

Ingredients:

- 1-pound fresh green beans, trimmed
- 2 tbsp butter
- 1 clove garlic, minced
- ¼ cup sliced almonds, toasted
- Salt and pepper

Directions:

1. Blanch beans in boiling water for 3–4 minutes. Drain.
2. Melt the butter, sauté the garlic, add the beans, and season to taste.
3. Toss, then sprinkle with almonds before serving.

BUTTER-STEWED CABBAGE

Skill Level: Easy
Prep Time: 10 minutes
Cook Time: 20 minutes
Total Time: 30 minutes
Yield: Serves 4

Ingredients:

- 1 medium green cabbage, shredded
- 3 tbsp butter
- ½ cup broth (vegetable or chicken)
- Salt and black pepper
- Pinch nutmeg (optional)

Directions:

1. Boil cabbage briefly until just tender. Drain.
2. In a pan, melt the butter, then add the cabbage, broth, and seasoning.
3. Simmer gently until it is tender and flavorful.

SOUPS & STEWS

SOUPS AND STEWS

Bread may have been the daily staple of the colonial diet, but it was the pot of soup that provided warmth, comfort, and community. In most homes, a kettle hung over the fire from dawn until dark, simmering with whatever could be spared. Bones, salted meat, root vegetables, and herbs were transformed into broths that stretched to feed families, neighbors, and weary travelers alike.

For soldiers and wanderers, soup was often the difference between hunger and survival. The Continental Army made do with thin broths of beef or pork, flavored only with onions, carrots, or cabbage—practical meals, easy to cook in bulk, and kept warm for hours on the hearth.

Regional traditions gave each pot its own character. In New England, fish chowder became a favorite: layers of cod or haddock, steeped with pork fat, onions, and hardtack crackers, were slowly stewed in water or milk. In the South, cooks prepared pepper pot stew—a spirited blend of beef tripe, greens, and hot peppers—a dish so beloved it would later become a winter staple in Philadelphia. Indigenous influence ran deep as well: many families drew upon Native traditions, combining corn, beans, and squash into stews that were as nourishing as they were economical.

A tavern bowl of chowder, a soldier's ration of broth, a family's cabbage soup—all carried the same purpose: to nourish and to comfort. Seasonings were simple—a pinch of salt, a bit of pepper, perhaps a sprig of thyme from the kitchen garden—but the satisfaction was universal. In years of scarcity and war, a steaming pot offered more than sustenance. It offered fellowship, a sense of home, and a quiet strength that helped carry the Revolution through its hardest winters.

HERCULES' ASPARAGUS SOUP

In April 1791, Dr. James McHenry sent George Washington a gift of refinement: fresh, hot-house asparagus. When the ground outside was still frozen, such early vegetables signaled not only the arrival of spring but also status and botanical mastery. Their correspondence reminds us that food could embody power as much as sustenance.

From that gift came a dish of asparagus soup. At Mount Vernon and in Philadelphia, enslaved cooks such as Hercules Posey—Washington's renowned chef—transformed seasonal produce into elegant fare. Salt pork, cream, and a delicate roux reflected English tradition; the sieving of vegetables into smoothness and the garnishing with tender tips revealed French influence. Every detail spoke of refinement. Yet that refinement rested upon enslaved labor. Hercules's artistry was celebrated throughout Washington's household, even as he remained in bondage—serving meals to a table where liberty was praised but not practiced.

On February 22, 1797, on Washington's sixty-fifth birthday, Hercules escaped from Mount Vernon. Washington sought his return, but Hercules was never found. He vanished into a young republic still struggling to define what freedom would mean.

This asparagus soup—once a symbol of elegance at the nation's first table—is offered here in both its historic and modern forms. May each bowl carry with it the memory of those who cooked in silence, yet helped shape the nation's taste.

Original Receipt

Boil asparagus stalks, onion, salt, pork, and pepper in broth for 1 hr. Strain the liquid, then press the pulp through a sieve. Return to the heat, add the reserved asparagus tips, and simmer. Stir in a butter-flour roux. Add cream. Simmer briefly. Serve hot.

Modern Recipe

Skill Level: Moderate
Prep Time: 15 minutes
Cook Time: 30 minutes
Total Time: 45 minutes
Yield: Serves 4 - 6

HERCULES' ASPARAGUS SOUP (Continued)

Ingredients

- 6 cups of chicken broth
- ½ cup diced salt pork or bacon
- 1 medium onion, chopped
- ¼ tsp white pepper
- 3 tbsp unsalted butter
- 3 tbsp all-purpose flour
- ¾ cup heavy cream or half and half
- Salt and pepper to taste
- 2 pounds of asparagus, trimmed
- Chopped chives or parsley to garnish

Directions

1. Cut stalks into 1-inch pieces. Reserve the tips for later.
2. Sauté base: Cook salt pork over medium heat until slightly crispy.
3. Add the onion and cook until softened.
4. Simmer the soup: Add asparagus stalks (not tips) and broth.
5. Bring to a boil, then reduce to a simmer and cook until the asparagus is tender, about 20 minutes.
6. Blend: Remove from heat. Purée the mixture.
7. Make a roux: In a small saucepan, melt butter over medium heat.
8. Stir in flour and cook, whisking constantly, for 1–2 minutes to remove raw taste. Thicken the soup: Return puréed soup to medium heat. Stir in the roux, whisking to combine. Add cream and reserved asparagus tips. Simmer for another 5–10 minutes, until the tips are tender and the soup has thickened slightly.

GREEN PEA SOUP

The American Revolution was not fought only on the battlefields of muskets and bayonets. It was endured in silence, behind locked hatches, aboard the rotting prison ships anchored in New York Harbor. The most infamous of these, the *Jersey*, was known as "Hell Afloat." Within its decaying timbers, thousands of captured soldiers and sailors languished in foul air, their names carved into the wood as if to outlast the suffering of their bodies.

Among the meager rations offered to them was pea soup. Survivors later wrote of it with a mixture of bitterness and gratitude: a thin green broth—sometimes little more than peas boiled in brackish water, sometimes laced with worms or grit from the barrel. It was scarcely a meal, yet for men wasted by hunger, it stood between another sunrise and the grave.

One former prisoner remembered, *"We clutched at it as if it were salvation, though it had neither taste nor nourishment."* Another recalled the cruel paradox—that the soup could not sustain life, yet the hope of it somehow kept them alive.

To tell the story of pea soup in the Revolution is to face its contradictions. In one place, it was hearty and sustaining, a dish of comfort and fellowship. In another, it was thin gruel, ladled out in darkness to men who would never taste freedom again. Both truths must be remembered. To lift a spoon of pea soup today is to honor not only the tables of the free, but also the hunger of the imprisoned— for both shaped the cost of independence.

Original Receipt

Take a quart of split peas, put them into five quarts of water, with a pound of lean beef, a pound of lean bacon, half an ounce of whole pepper, a bundle of sweet herbs, a large onion, a carrot; cover them close, and let them boil two hours. Then strain it through a coarse sieve, and put it into the saucepan again, with a piece of carrot and turnip cut small, and a head of celery; season with salt and let them boil till tender. Fry some small bits of bread until crisp, then put them into the dish.

GREEN PEA SOUP (Continued)

Modern Recipe

Skill Level: Easy
Prep Time: 15 minutes
Cook Time: 75 minutes
Total Time: 1 hour 30 minutes
Yield: Serves 6

Ingredients

- 2 tbsp olive oil or butter
- 1 large onion, diced
- 2 carrots, diced
- 2 celery stalks, diced
- 3 garlic cloves, minced
- 1 pound dried split peas, rinsed
- 2 tbsp fresh parsley, chopped
- 6 cups chicken or vegetable stock
- 1 smoked ham hock *or* 2 cups diced ham
- 2 bay leaves
- 1 tbsp dried thyme
- Salt to taste
- Optional garnish: cream, olive oil, or bacon bits

Directions

1. In a Dutch oven, heat olive oil or butter over medium heat.
2. Add onion, carrot, and celery. Cook until softened, 6–7 minutes.
3. Stir in garlic and cook 1 minute more.
4. Add split peas, stock, ham hock (if using), bay leaves, thyme, salt, and pepper. Bring to boil.

5. Reduce the heat to low, cover partially, and simmer gently for 60–75 minutes, stirring occasionally to prevent sticking.

6. Remove Bay leaves and ham hock. Shred meat from the hock and return to the pot.

7. For a smooth soup, blend with a blender. For rustic style, leave it chunky.

8. Taste and adjust seasoning. Serve with bread and fresh parsley.

BARLEY AND BEAN SOUP

On a blistering June day in 1778, the Battle of Monmouth raged beneath the New Jersey sun. Mary Ludwig Hays—remembered in history as Molly Pitcher—ran across the battlefield with buckets of water to cool the cannons and quench the thirst of the men. When her husband collapsed beside his gun, she stepped into his place, loading and firing under enemy fire. For that act of courage, she became a symbol of the Revolution's resolve.

Yet away from the smoke and roar of battle, women like Molly sustained the cause in quieter ways. As "camp followers," they cooked, mended, and nursed, transforming meager provisions into nourishment. Barley and beans were staples—filling, inexpensive, and easy to stretch for many mouths. Diaries from the camps speak of kettles of barley broth, thickened with peas or beans, ladled out to exhausted soldiers after battle.

Molly Pitcher's name endures as the woman with the water bucket. But her hands—like those of countless women whose names were never recorded—also stirred kettles of barley and beans, offering warmth and strength when liberty's flame burned low. To taste this soup today is to honor those women whose courage was measured not only in the thunder of cannon, but in the quiet labor of the campfire.

Original Receipt

Take half a pound of pearl barley, wash it in three or four waters, put it into a stew-pan with a knuckle of veal, or shin of beef, or a piece of mutton, and put in a gallon of water, with a crust of bread toasted brown, two or three onions, a bundle of sweet herbs, a little pepper, a turnip and carrot; cover close, and let it boil softly two hours, then strain it off, put in the barley again, with some dried peas, or French beans cut small, and let it boil softly till the peas are done; then season with salt.

Modern Recipe

Skill Level: Easy
Prep Time: 15 minutes
Cook Time: 60 - 75 minutes
Total Time: 1 hour 30 minutes
Yield: Serves 6- 8

BARLEY AND BEAN SOUP (Continued)

Ingredients

- 2 tbsp olive oil
- 1 cup pearl barley, rinsed
- 1 onion, diced
- 1 cup dried beans (great northern, or black-eyed), soaked overnight
- 2 carrots, diced
- 8 cups of vegetables or chicken stock
- 2 celery stalks, diced
- 2 bay leaves
- 3 garlic cloves, minced
- 1 tsp dried thyme
- 1 smoked turkey leg *or* ham bone (optional)
- 1 tsp salt (to taste)
- ½ tsp black pepper
- 2 tbsp fresh parsley, chopped

Directions

1. Heat oil in a large pot over medium heat.
2. Add the onion, carrot, and celery and sauté until soft, about 6 minutes.
3. Add garlic; cook 1 minute.
4. Stir in barley and soaked beans.
5. Pour in the stock and add the bay leaves, thyme, pepper, and smoked meat, if using.
6. Bring to a boil, then reduce the heat. Simmer gently 60–75 minutes, stirring occasionally, until beans and barley are tender.
7. Remove bay leaves and bone.
8. Taste and adjust, stir in parsley, and serve.

FRENCH ONION SOUP

In the summer of 1781, the French army under General Rochambeau left Rhode Island and began its long march through Connecticut. It was no ordinary column. Twelve miles of white coats and glinting bayonets wound through Yankee villages—a river of soldiers moving south to join Washington in a final gamble for independence. Farmers, housewives, and children stood silently at their gates, watching a sight few had ever imagined: French soldiers, allies now, marching for the same cause.

The march was not without hardship. The French were strangers in a land of suspicion. Some villagers feared plunder; others doubted whether Catholic soldiers could be trusted. What softened that tension was food. In the town of Bolton, Connecticut, French officers invited local families to their campfires. From iron kettles rose the fragrance of onions fried in butter, simmered in broth, and ladled over bread.

Diaries tell us that Americans were struck by the "savory vapors of their pots." Most colonial soups were plain and thin; this was a revelation—onions turned to sweetness; bread softened into comfort. For many, it was their first encounter with Old World cookery, not read about in books but steaming from the campfires of their new allies.

That night, as villagers dipped bread into bowls of *soupe à l'oignon*, suspicion gave way to laughter. They could not share a language, but they shared a meal. In the months ahead, those same soldiers would march to Yorktown, their bayonets gleaming beside Washington's. Victory would be sealed by cannon and treaty—but trust began in quieter ways, over the humble sweetness of onions simmering in a French pot.

<u>Original Receipt</u>

Slice onions very thin and fry them in butter until lightly browned. Add broth, a little salt, and simmer together. Place toasted bread slices in the bottom of a dish, pour the onion soup over them, and serve very hot.

FRENCH ONION SOUP (Continued)

Modern Recipe

Skill Level: Moderate
Prep Time: 15 minutes
Cook Time: 60 minutes
Total Time: 1 hour 15 minutes
Yield: Serves 6

Ingredients

- 4 large yellow onions, thinly sliced
- 8 cups beef or vegetable stock
- 3 tbsp unsalted butter
- 1 bay leaf
- 2 tbsp of olive oil
- ½ tsp dried thyme (or sprigs fresh)
- 2 garlic cloves, minced
- ½ tsp black pepper
- 1 tsp sugar (for caramelizing)
- 1 tsp salt (to taste)
- ½ cup dry white wine (optional)
- 1 baguette, sliced and toasted
- 2 cups grated Gruyère or Swiss cheese

Directions

1. Melt butter and oil in a heavy pot. Add onions, sugar, and a pinch of salt. Cook over medium-low heat, stirring often, until golden brown (30–40 minutes).

2. Stir in the garlic and white wine (if using), scraping up the browned bits. Cook until the wine is reduced by half.

3. Add stock, bay leaf, thyme, salt, and pepper. Simmer uncovered for 30 minutes. Remove the bay leaf.

FRENCH ONION SOUP (Continued)

4.   Toast baguette slices under a broiler until crisp.

5.   Ladle soup into bowls, top with toasted bread and cheese.

6.   Broil until the cheese is melted, bubbling, and lightly browned.

CHICKEN NOODLE SOUP

In the autumn of 1777, after the battles of Brandywine and Germantown, wagonloads of wounded men rattled into the quiet Moravian town of Bethlehem, Pennsylvania. Its communal halls, once filled with hymns and prayer, were transformed overnight into military hospitals. The sisters of the community—German women bound by faith, discipline, and mercy—suddenly found themselves at the front lines of a different kind of war.

Their diaries tell of long days and longer nights: washing wounds, boiling linens, sitting beside men lost in fever. But they also cooked. From the kitchens of the Sisters' House rose the scent of a dish both humble and profound—*nudel suppe*, noodle soup. Chickens from local farms, onions and cabbage from the garden, flour worked into dough and cut into thin strips—all simmered together into steaming bowls carried to soldiers too weak to stand.

To many Anglo-American troops, it was an unfamiliar taste. Noodles were still rare in English kitchens, but for the German sisters, they were the flavor of home—nourishment carried across the ocean in memory and tradition. One visitor remarked on the "strange pastes" floating in broth; others marveled that such food could be both filling and tender, a comfort in a foreign tongue.

It is no accident that chicken noodle soup remains our comfort food to this day. When fevers rise, or spirits falter, we reach for the same warm bowl that once soothed broken soldiers—proof that compassion, like flavor, can cross any border and endure through generations.

<u>Original Receipt</u>

Take flour and a little water, with an egg or two, work it into a stiff paste, roll it thin, and cut it into narrow slips, or in little pieces, as you please. They may be put into broth and will make it both hearty and good.

<u>Modern Recipe</u>

Skill Level: Easy
Prep Time: 20 minutes
Cook Time: 1 hour 30 minutes
Total Time: 1 hour 50 minutes

CHICKEN NOODLE SOUP (Continued)

Yield: Serves 6 - 8

Ingredients

- 1 whole chicken (about 3–4 pounds cut into pieces)
- 2 carrots, diced
- 10 cups of water or chicken stock
- 2 celery stalks, diced
- 2 bay leaves
- ½ small head of green cabbage, shredded
- 1 onion, quartered
- 8 oz egg noodles (or homemade)
- 3 garlic cloves, smashed
- 1 tsp salt (to taste)
- 1 tsp black pepper
- 2 tbsp fresh parsley, chopped

Directions

1. In a large pot, combine the chicken, water or stock, bay leaves, onion, garlic, pepper, and salt.
2. Bring to a boil, then reduce the heat and simmer for 1 hour, skimming foam as needed.
3. Remove the chicken and set it aside to cool slightly. Strain the broth, discard the solids, and return the broth to the pot.
4. Add carrots, celery, and cabbage. Simmer 20 minutes
5. Stir in noodles and cook until just tender, 8–10 minutes.
6. Remove the meat from the bones, shred it, and return it to the soup. Adjust seasoning.
7. Stir in fresh parsley. Serve hot with crusty bread.

PIES & PASTRIES

PIES AND PASTRIES

In the eighteenth century, a "pie" did not mean what it does today. We picture flaky apple pies cooling on windowsills, or pumpkin pies spiced with cinnamon and nutmeg. But in Revolutionary America, pies and pastries were often a matter of endurance rather than indulgence.

A pie was first and foremost a container. Its crust—sometimes called a "coffin"—was thick, heavy, and designed to preserve meat, fish, or vegetables for days at a time. Inside might be beef and onions, pigeon and pork, or venison stewed with ale. These hearty, savory pies sustained households through long winters and fed soldiers on the march. Sweet pies did exist—apple, pumpkin, and custard—but they were rare, prepared for holidays or when sugar and imported spices could be spared.

Pastry was both a necessity and an art. In wealthier homes, the table might boast a latticed tart filled with quince or a raised pie shaped like a sculpture. In taverns, simpler hand-pies were sold to travelers, their crusts thick enough to survive the road. Enslaved cooks prepared fine pastries for their masters, while crafting humbler versions for themselves from scraps. For women, skill in pastry-making was a mark of pride and reputation—something handed down in receipt books and remembered long after the names of battles had faded.

To us, pastry means sweetness, comfort, and dessert. To them, it meant preservation, sustenance, and often status. Yet across the centuries, pies have carried the same quiet promise: to gather people around a table, to mark the passing of seasons, to turn what one has into something meant to be shared.

MINCED BEEF PIE

In the winter of 1777, while Washington's men shivered at Valley Forge, General Sir William Howe presided over Philadelphia. The city had fallen to British arms, and its streets filled with red coats and Loyalist revelry. In Parliament and in the pamphlets of the day, Howe was accused of indulgence—of choosing comfort over campaign.

His officers dined well: roasts, puddings, wine, and pies. At their tables, minced beef pies flavored with dried fruit and Madeira carried the taste of Britain into occupied America. These were not the rough rations of common soldiers—salt pork, hard bread, and thin broth—but the fare of gentlemen at ease in the midst of war.

Howe's critics called him careless, too fond of luxury in a city that offered it freely. Yet perhaps the minced beef pie, served steaming in the drawing rooms of Philadelphia, tells us something of the war itself. For the Patriots, pies were carried cold in pockets or eaten hastily in taverns—fuel for men always on the move. For Howe's officers, pastry was not a necessity but a display: a reminder of the world they fought to preserve.

The contrast is striking—one pie, two meanings. A symbol of indulgence at the British table, and of endurance in the Patriot camp. Both crusts baked in the same century's ovens, both holding within them the taste and tension of a Revolution.

Original Receipt

Take of cold roast beef, mince it small, add to it some currants, chopped apples, a little suet, with nutmeg and cloves. Moisten with a glass of red wine or sack. Lay it in a good crust and bake well.

Modern Recipe

Skill Level: Moderate
Prep Time: 30 minutes
Cook Time: 25 minutes
Total Time: 55 minutes
Yield: 8 – 10 hand pies

MINCED BEEF PIE (Continued)

Ingredients

- 2 tbsp butter or olive oil
- 1 cup chopped apple
- 1 pound ground beef
- ½ cup raisins or currants
- 1 small onion, finely diced
- ½ tsp ground nutmeg
- 2 garlic cloves, minced
- ½ tsp ground cloves
- 1 tsp salt
- ½ cup red wine (or apple cider)
- ½ tsp black pepper
- 1 package of puff pastry (or homemade)

Directions

1. Heat butter in a skillet. Sauté the onion and garlic until soft.
2. Add the ground beef and cook until browned.
3. Stir in the apple, raisins, currants, nutmeg, cloves, salt, pepper, and wine. Simmer until thickened, for about 10 minutes. Let cool slightly.
4. Prepare the pastry: roll the puff pastry and cut into 4–5-inch circles.
5. Place a spoonful of filling in the center. Fold over and crimp the edges with a fork.
6. Arrange on a baking sheet, brush tops with beaten egg.
7. Bake at 400°F (200°C) for 20–25 minutes, until golden.
8. Best warm. These may be eaten by hand, as soldiers once did.

APPLE TART

They called him "Gentleman Johnny." In 1777, General John Burgoyne marched south from Canada with an army of seven thousand men—and a baggage train that glittered like a traveling court. His wagons carried wine and delicacies, silver service and fine linens, uniforms for every occasion, even costumes for evenings of theater.

But the wilderness of northern New York was merciless. The army hacked roads through forest and swamp, built bridges across bogs, and dragged its cannon mile by mile. The baggage wagons slowed to a crawl, and hunger began to gnaw. Rations dwindled, salted meat spoiled, and bread ran out.

Across the lines, American militia lived differently. They foraged the countryside, sustained by the generosity of farm families whose orchards that autumn hung heavy with apples. In brick ovens and iron kettles, those apples were sliced and sweetened with maple syrup or molasses when sugar could not be found, then laid into simple crusts. Rustic tarts emerged from farmhouse hearths—plain, sustaining, and deeply familiar.

When Burgoyne was surrounded at Saratoga and forced to surrender, his glittering baggage train became a symbol of folly—too heavy, too indulgent, too far from the soil of the land he hoped to master. The apple tart, by contrast, born from the orchards of New York and baked by rough hands in modest kitchens, stood as a quiet emblem of resilience. At Saratoga, indulgence met its end, and simplicity prevailed. The general's silver cooled in defeat, while the scent of apple and spice rose from the hearths of the victors.

<u>Original Receipt</u>

Pare and quarter apples, take out the cores, stew them with a little water, a bit of lemon-peel, and some sugar, till soft. Mash and put them into a tart case, with a little cinnamon and butter; then bake it. Or lay thin slices of raw apple in your tart, with sugar between the layers, and bake till done.

APPLE TART (Continued)

Modern Recipe

Skill Level: Easy
Prep Time: 20 minutes
Cook Time: 35 – 40 minutes
Total Time: 1 hour
Yield: Serves 6 - 8

Ingredients

- 1 package of puff pastry (or homemade short crust)
- 2 tbsp butter, melted
- 5 medium apples, peeled and sliced thin
- 2 tbsp maple syrup (or brown sugar)
- 1 tsp lemon zest
- ½ tsp cinnamon
- 1 tbsp lemon juice
- Pinch nutmeg
- 1 egg, beaten (for egg wash)
- Powdered sugar (optional)

Directions

1. Toss apple slices with lemon juice, zest, maple syrup, cinnamon, and nutmeg.

2. Roll the pastry into a 10–12-inch circle. Arrange apples on the pastry, drizzle with melted butter, fold the edges in a rustic style, and brush the crust with egg.

3. Bake at 400°F (200°C) for 35–40 minutes, until golden brown.

4. Serve – Warm or room temperature, dusted with sugar.

CUSTARD TART

In the autumn of 1781, British General Charles Cornwallis found himself besieged at Yorktown. For weeks, cannon fire rained down as French and American troops drew their lines tighter. Inside the British camp, supplies dwindled, soldiers weakened, and desperation took hold. Yet for Cornwallis and his officers, the habits of refinement were never far away.

Custard tarts—eggs, cream, sugar, and a dusting of nutmeg baked in delicate pastry shells—were familiar fare at the tables of British officers. Recipes for them appeared in English cookbooks across the Atlantic, symbols of order and civilization in an age of chaos. To serve a custard tart was to affirm one's station, to preserve the manners of gentility even as the empire trembled.

But refinement could not withstand reality. At Yorktown, the world of silver spoons and custard tarts collided with the roar of artillery. Cornwallis's surrender marked more than a military defeat; it was the collapse of British dominion in America. The custard tart—refined, fragile, and sweet—stood in stark contrast to the bitterness of the moment: officers dining on cream and spice while soldiers gnawed on salt meat. And when Cornwallis's sword was offered in surrender, no pastry could soften the taste of defeat.

<u>Original Receipt</u>

Boil a pint of cream with a little cinnamon, then take out the spice. Beat up the yolks of five eggs with a spoonful of rosewater and sweeten to taste. Stir into the cream and pour into a dish lined with paste. Bake till set and grate nutmeg over.

Modern Recipe

Skill Level: Easy
Prep Time: 20 minutes
Cook Time: 45 minutes
Total Time: 1 hour 5 minutes
Yield: Serves 6 -8

Ingredients

- 1 pie crust (homemade or store-bought)

- 1 tsp vanilla extract (or 1 tsp rosewater)

CUSTARD TART (Continued)

- 2 cups heavy cream (or milk)
- ½ tsp cinnamon (or small cinnamon stick)
- 5 egg yolks
- ¼ tsp nutmeg (grated)
- ½ cup sugar

Pinch salt

Directions

1. Prepare the crust: Line a 9-inch tart pan with pastry. Prick the base with a fork and blind-bake at 375°F (190°C) for 12 minutes. Remove from the oven.
2. In a saucepan, gently heat the cream with the cinnamon stick over medium-low heat until it begins to steam. Do not boil. Remove from heat and discard the cinnamon stick.
3. In a bowl, whisk together the egg yolks, sugar, vanilla (or rosewater), and a pinch of salt. Whisk in the warm cream slowly to temper the eggs.
4. Reduce the oven temperature to 325°F (160°C). Pour the custard into the prepared crust and grate nutmeg lightly over the top.
5. Bake for 25–30 minutes, until the custard is just set around the edges but still slightly wobbly in the center.
6. Remove from the oven and allow to cool slightly before slicing. Serve warm or chilled.

BEEF STEAK PIE

The floor of Tun Tavern creaked beneath the weight of men and the burden of secrets. The air was thick with wood smoke, yeast, and meat gravy—beef steak pies pulled fresh from the hearth. Tankards of dark colonial ale clanked upon the tables. Outside, the Delaware River lapped cold against the docks, but inside, the heat of history was rising.

Captain Samuel Nicholas, Quaker-born, sat close by the fire. Around him gathered a circle of fishermen, tradesmen, and former British Marines. The pie before them steamed softly. The ale burned warm in their chests.

Nicholas cleared his throat. "Men," he said, "this isn't about empire or king. It's about liberty. It's about a new order—forged by us. I need fighters. Not just soldiers—Marines."

Tun Tavern, founded nearly a century before, had hosted Masons and Freemasons, patriots and poets. But never this—the birth of a fighting force sworn not to a crown, but to a cause. A force that would cross seas, scale barricades, and fire from the rails of ships beneath a new striped flag.

By midnight, the first names were inked. Thirty-one men walked out of Tun Tavern and into the pages of American history. They did not know what lay ahead, only that they had been fed, warmed, and called to something greater. The next morning, the fire had burned low, the pie dish was empty—and the United States Marine Corps had been born.

Original Receipt

Take slices of beef, roll in flour, and season with salt, pepper, and a little nutmeg; lay in paste No. 1. with small bits of butter, add a few potatoes, if handy, or slices of onion, a little water, and a paste over the top. Bake one and half hour."

Modern Recipe

Skill Level: Moderate
Prep Time: 30 minutes
Cook Time: 2 hours
Total Time: 2 ½ hours
Yield: Serves 6 -8

BEEF STEAK PIE (Continued)

Ingredients

- 2 pounds stew meat cut into 1-inch cubes
- 1 large yellow onion, thinly sliced
- 2 cloves garlic, minced
- 1 cup mushrooms, sliced
- 2 tbsp flour
- 1 tbsp butter or beef drippings
- 1 cup dark ale (porter or brown ale, preferably English Style)
- ½ cup beef stock
- 1 tbsp Worcestershire sauce (or anchovy-based sauce)
- ½ tsp cracked black pepper
- 1 tsp salt
- 1 pie crust (top only, or bottom and top if preferred)
- 1 egg yolk mixed with 1 tbsp water for egg wash

Directions

1. In a Dutch oven or large skillet, heat butter or fat. Sear beef in batches until browned. Set aside.

2. Sauté the onions and mushrooms until tender, adding the garlic in the final minute.

3. Sprinkle in the flour and stir until the mixture is well-coated. Slowly pour in ale and stock, scraping up bits. Add Worcestershire sauce, mustard, thyme, salt, and pepper.

4. Return beef to the pot. Cover and simmer for 1.5–2 hours, until the meat is tender and the sauce has thickened.

5. Preheat oven to 375°F (190°C). Place filling in a pie dish. Cover with crust, seal edges, and cut steam vents.

6. Brush crust with egg wash. Bake 35–45 min, until golden brown and bubbling.

7. Let it sit for 10 minutes before slicing.

SWEET POTATO PIE

By the winter of 1776, Long Island lay under British control. The soldiers did not knock. They entered civilian homes without invitation or permission. To resist was perilous. To protest, fatal.

In one such home lived Grace Barclay. Her house was spared from fire, but it was no longer hers alone. British officers quartered there— sleeping in her rooms, eating from her family's table, watching her children at play.

Grace kept a journal. In one entry, later preserved by Lydia Post, she wrote only a few words: *"Sweet potato pudding, and more."* No embellishment. No sentiment. Just the plain record of a meal cooked under supervision. Yet that single line tells us everything.

The pudding—what we would call sweet potato pie—was more than food. It was memory, tradition, and comfort baked into uncertain days. Recipes like hers were not written but remembered, passed from one generation to the next, and adapted to whatever the pantry could provide. Sugar was rationed. Spices were scarce. Still, she baked. And in its own quiet way, that act was resistance.

Perhaps she made it to ease a tense table, to remind her children that life could still feel familiar. There was no toast raised over the pie, no declaration signed beside it. It was eaten in a house no longer free. Yet that simple dish endures—proof that even under occupation, they lived, they remembered, and they continued to cook.

Original Receipt

Boil one pound of sweet potatoes very tender, rub them while hot through a colander; add six eggs well beaten, three quarters of a pound of powdered sugar, three quarters of butter, and some grated nutmeg and lemon peel, with a glass of brandy; put a paste in the dish, and when the pudding is done.

Modern Recipe

Skill Level: Easy
Prep Time: 20 minutes
Cook Time: 45 – 50 minutes
Total Time: 1 hour 10 minutes
Yield: 1 (9-inch) pie

SWEET POTATO PIE (Continued)

Ingredients

- 1 unbaked 9-inch pie shell
- 2 medium sweet potatoes, roasted and mashed (~2 cups)
- ¾ cup brown sugar
- ½ cup milk or evaporated milk
- 2 eggs
- 4 tbsp butter, melted
- 1 tsp cinnamon
- ½ tsp nutmeg
- ½ tsp ginger (optional)
- 1 tsp vanilla (or brandy)
- pinch salt

Directions

1. Preheat oven to 375°F
2. Mix all ingredients until smooth. Pour into the prepared pie shell.
3. Bake for 45–50 minutes, or until the center is set, still slightly soft.
4. Cool before slicing. Serve with whipped cream.

MEATS &
MAIN DISHES

MEAT AND MAIN DISHES

In colonial America, no meal was truly complete without meat. It stood at the heart of the table—symbolizing survival, abundance, and hospitality. For those who could afford it, roasted or stewed meats signaled comfort and prosperity. For soldiers in the field, a simple slice of salted beef or pork could mean the difference between strength and hunger.

During the American Revolution (1775–1783), shortages and British blockades often determined what ended up on the plate. Yet, even in the hardest of times, meat remained the centerpiece of most meals—proof of both resourcefulness and resilience.

Salted pork and beef were staples, especially for the Continental Army. Packed tightly in barrels, the cuts were briny, challenging, and far from tender—but essential for sustaining soldiers on long marches. At home, families would boil or stew these same cuts with whatever vegetables were available, softening the salt and stretching the meal to feed more mouths.

When fresh meat was available, it transformed the table into a place of celebration. Roast beef, venison, or mutton often marked a special occasion in wealthier homes or taverns. A joint of beef or a leg of mutton roasted before the fire and basted with its own drippings was considered a mark of pride and good fortune. In the southern colonies, ham cured with molasses or smoked over hickory fires filled kitchens with a rich, smoky sweetness, often served alongside cornmeal mush or tender greens. Poultry, too, was treasured: goose or turkey for holidays, and chicken for everyday meals—frequently stuffed with apples, onions, or chestnuts.

For those living near rivers and forests, the land itself provided. Rabbits, squirrels, ducks, and partridges filled pots and pans; nothing went to waste. Bones, flavored broths and gravies, and even leftovers, found new life as fillings for pies or pastries. Seasonings were simple but purposeful: salt, pepper, mustard, vinegar, and, when available, imported spices like nutmeg or cloves added warmth to otherwise humble fare.

Main dishes in the Revolutionary era were seldom elaborate, yet they carried deep meaning. Around smoky campfires, soldiers shared rations of salted pork; in family kitchens, roasts turned slowly before open hearths; in taverns, hearty joints of beef were carved for travelers and townsfolk alike. Each meal told a story—of endurance, community, and the will to thrive through scarcity.

In every form, meat nourished more than the body—it fed the spirit of a people. From battlefield camps to farmhouse kitchens, it sustained both household and army through years of hunger, hardship, and hope. In the simple act of preparing and sharing meat, early Americans found strength, identity, and the taste of a nation being born.

ROAST BEEF OF OLD ENGLAND

In the age of the American Revolution, roast beef was more than supper—it was a ceremony. In England, King George III dined on it at court, carved it at royal banquets, and served it with horseradish and gravy. In occupied America, Loyalist families in New York and Philadelphia laid it before British generals, basted it in butter, served it on fine china, and washed it down with Madeira wine.

A rib roast cost three to four pence a pound in 1775—far beyond the reach of most colonists. And so the dish became a symbol of power and privilege. For the officer's mess, it was pride and tradition. For Washington's men, gnawing fire cakes at Valley Forge, it was a memory of arrogance—mocked in the streets whenever the anthem *"The Roast Beef of Old England"* was sung. In Boston taverns, Loyalists sang that same tune while raising their tankards. Patriots whistled it back in reply—the melody turned from anthem to insult, the song of empire remade as defiance.

Original Receipt

To roast a rib of beef. Spat it right, rub with flour, baste with fat, and add a little salt and water. When done, baste with butter and dredge with flour to froth. Serve with strong gravy and garnish with horseradish.

Modern Recipe

Skill Level: Moderate
Prep Time: 20 minutes
Cook Time: 1 hour 15 minutes to 1 hour and 30 minutes
Total Time: 1 hour 45 minutes
Yield: Serves 6 -8

Ingredients

- 1 rib roast, 4–6 pounds

- 2 tbsp flour

- 2 tbsp butter

- 1 cup beef stock

- salt and pepper

- Fresh horseradish or horseradish cream

ROAST BEEF OF OLD ENGLAND (Continued)

Directions

1. Preheat oven to 375°F (190°C).

2. Rub roast with flour, salt, and pepper.

3. Place on a rack in a roasting pan; cook for 15–20 minutes per pound, basting with butter and drippings.

4. For medium-rare, remove at 130–135°F and let rest for 15 minutes.

5. Make gravy: Whisk the flour into the pan drippings over medium heat. Gradually add the stock, whisking constantly, until the gravy thickens and bubbles.

6. Slice and serve with gravy.

7. Serve with horseradish or horseradish cream and roasted vegetables, or with Yorkshire pudding for authenticity.

Figure 3. O the Roast Beef of Old England

MARY RANDOLPH'S FRIED CHICKEN

Mary Randolph once dined with presidents. She was born to silver spoons and enslaved servants, raised among Virginia's first families. But by 1824, all that was gone. Her husband had lost his post after speaking too freely against their cousin—President Thomas Jefferson. The mansion emptied, debts mounted, and the Randolphs fell so swiftly that people whispered their disgrace in the markets.

So Mary did something remarkable. She began to cook.

In a small, sweltering kitchen in Washington City, she salvaged what she could: a few old pans, one good dress, and the help of the enslaved women who worked beside her—women whose skill and endurance would sustain them all.

That night, she made fried chicken. Not the kind hastily slapped in a pan but prepared with the precision of a French chef. She cut the birds cleanly at the joints, dredged them in flour, and dropped them into boiling lard until they turned crisp, golden, and almost luminous. Alongside, she served fried mush—a humble dish—lifted with fresh parsley, sizzling green like confetti. Then came the gravy: milk, butter, salt, pepper, and more parsley, poured like silk. She did not let a servant serve it. She served it herself.

Every guest cleaned their plate. A senator asked for the recipe. No one mentioned the family's fall, or the scandal, or the shame. They just remembered the chicken.

A year later, Mary Randolph published *The Virginia Housewife*—the first American cookbook of its kind. It sold out quickly. That fried chicken, born of necessity and pride, fed her family, restored her name, and turned a Southern downfall into an American legend.

Original Receipt

Cut them up as for the fricassee, dredge them well with flour, sprinkle them with salt, put them into a good quantity of boiling lard, and fry them a light brown; fry small pieces of mush and a quantity of parsley nicely picked, to be served in the dish with the chickens; take half a pint of rich milk, add to it a small bit of butter, with

MARY RANDOLPH'S FRIED CHICKEN (Continued)

pepper, salt, and chopped parsley; stew it a little, and pour it over the chicken, and then garnish with the fried parsley.

Modern Recipe

Skill Level: Moderate
Prep Time: 25 minutes
Cook Time: 35 – 40 minutes
Total Time: 1 hour and 5 minutes
Yield: Serves 4 - 6

Ingredients

- 1 whole chicken cut into eight pieces

- 1 tsp kosher salt

- ½ tsp black pepper

- ½ tsp garlic powder

- ½ tsp onion powder

- ¼ tsp paprika

- 1½ cups all-purpose flour

- lard or vegetable oil

Directions

1. Season the chicken and pat it dry. In a small bowl, mix salt, pepper, garlic powder, onion powder, and paprika. Rub onto chicken pieces.

2. Cut the chicken into eight parts (two breasts, two thighs, two drumsticks, two wings).

3. Dredge in Flour: Place flour in a shallow dish and coat chicken thoroughly. After dredging, let the chicken rest for 10 minutes to help the flour adhere and form a crisp crust.

4. Fry - heat the lard or oil to 350°F. Fry chicken in batches until golden brown and cooked through (internal temp: 165°F), about 15–18 minutes. Drain.

MARY RANDOLPH'S FRIED CHICKEN (Continued)

5. Make Gravy: In a saucepan, warm milk with 2 tablespoons butter, salt, pepper, and parsley. Simmer gently for 3–5 minutes.

6. Serve: Pour gravy lightly over chicken. Garnish with fried parsley and mush, if desired, and it is traditionally served with fried mush or spoonbread.

NANCY HART'S TURKEY

It was said that Nancy Hart stood barely five feet tall, but she towered in spirit. On the Georgia frontier during the Revolution, her log cabin stood as a lone outpost of Patriot resolve. One evening, a band of Loyalist soldiers—Tories—burst through the door. They demanded food, and they demanded it from her.

Nancy, never one to yield, nodded and drew a fat turkey from the yard. She plucked it, dressed it, and set it to roast over the hearth, the savory scent filling the small cabin. The men laughed and drank, growing careless—never noticing that as Nancy tended the fire, she was also slipping their muskets, one by one, through a crack in the wall to her young daughter waiting outside.

When one soldier caught her in the act and lunged for the weapons, Nancy seized a gun of her own. She leveled it with a steady hand and fired, killing him where he stood. The others froze. One by one, she held them at bay until neighbors arrived. By nightfall, the men who had demanded her turkey hung from a nearby tree, executed as spies.

The story spread, carried by word of mouth through a region where survival depended on nerve as much as arms. Whether every detail unfolded exactly as later told cannot be proven. But the world that produced the story is beyond doubt. On the Revolutionary frontier, kitchens were battlegrounds. Meals were moments of exposure. And a turkey — roasted patiently over an open fire — could become the center of a struggle for control, courage, and life itself.

Her story endures as both legend and warning—proof that courage may wear an apron, and that even a simple roasted turkey, golden and fragrant, can mark the turning of a nation's fate.

NANCY HART'S TURKEY (Continued)

<u>Original Receipt</u>

One pound soft wheat bread, three ounces beef suet, three eggs, a little sweet thyme, marjoram, pepper, and salt, and one wine glass of wine; fill the bird therewith and sew up, hang down to a steady solid fire, basting frequently with butter, and a little water; when done, garnish with parsley or fennel; serve up with boiled onions and gravy.

Modern Recipe

Skill Level: Moderate
Prep Time: 30 minutes
Cook Time: 3 - 3½ hours
Total Time: About 4 hours
Yield: Serves 8 - 10

Ingredients

- 1 whole turkey (10–12 pounds), thawed if frozen
- 1-pound fresh breadcrumbs (from rustic wheat bread)
- 4 tbsp melted butter
- 3 eggs, lightly beaten
- 1 tsp dried thyme
- 1 tsp dried marjoram (or oregano if unavailable)
- 1 tsp salt
- ½ tsp black pepper
- ½ cup dry white wine or apple cider
- fresh parsley or fennel (for garnish)

Directions

1. In a large bowl, mix breadcrumbs, softened butter, eggs, thyme, marjoram, salt, pepper, and wine until well combined and moistened.

2. Remove giblets, pat turkey dry, and fill the cavity with stuffing. Truss the legs or tie them together.

NANCY HART'S TURKEY (Continued)

3. Preheat oven to 325°F (165°C). Place the turkey on a rack in a roasting pan, breast side up. Brush with melted butter.

4. Roast about 15 minutes per pound (roughly 3–3½ hours for a 12-lb. bird), basting every 30 minutes. Tent with foil if browning too quickly.

5. Turkey is done when the internal temperature reaches 165°F (74°C). Let it rest 20 minutes before carving. Garnish with parsley.

SMOKED HAM WITH MOLASSES GLAZE

The East River stank of rot and seawater. In 1778, British prison ships bobbed off New York's coast—floating coffins where captured American soldiers lay starving, sick, and forgotten. And yet, through that stench and silence, came a woman.

Elizabeth Burgin, a widow with three children, brought what she could: food, bread, and meat—the kind that could keep a man alive one more day. She hid it beneath her cloak and slipped past redcoat eyes and gleaming bayonets. "The poor creatures," she recalled later, "looked on with such longing eyes." For them, a crust of bread was a sacrament. A slice of salted meat—ham, cured and portable—was hope made tangible.

She made dozens of such journeys before the British discovered her. A price was placed on her head. She fled into hiding, helped by the very cause she had nourished.

This dish—Smoked Ham with Molasses Glaze—honors her courage. Salted, cured, and slowly baked, it recalls the food she carried in secret, the sustenance she risked her life to give. The molasses glaze, added in peace, transforms survival into celebration. Once hidden under a cloak, now placed proudly at the center of the table, it reminds us that liberty was carried not only by generals and soldiers, but by women who bore bread and meat into the darkness—and fed a nation's hope.

<u>Original Receipt</u>

Soak the ham in water all night, scrape and wash it very clean, put it in a boiler with cold water, let it simmer, not boil, for two or three hours according to its size; take it out, pull off the skin, rub it over with yolk of egg, strew it thick with bread crumbs, put it in a Dutch oven to brown, or in a hot stove; garnish with green parsley, and serve it up.

<u>Modern Recipe</u>

Skill Level: Moderate

Prep Time: 20 minutes (plus soaking time if needed)

Cook Time: 3½ - 4 hours

Total Time: About 4 ½ hours

SMOKE HAM WITH MOLASSES GLAZE (Continued)

Yield: Serves 8 - 10

Ingredients

- 1 whole smoked ham (8–10 pounds), bone-in or boneless
- 1 cup molasses (blackstrap or mild)
- ½ cup brown sugar
- 2 tbsp Dijon mustard or ground mustard
- ¼ tsp clove (ground or whole cloves for studding)
- 1–2 cups breadcrumbs (optional, for crust)
- yolk of 1 egg (for sticking crumbs, as in Randolph's version)

Directions

1. If the ham is very salty or country-cured, soak it overnight in cold water to reduce excess salt. Drain well and pat dry.

2. Place in a large pot, cover with cold water, and simmer gently (don't boil) for 2–3 hours, depending on size.

3. In a saucepan, combine molasses, brown sugar, mustard, and clove. Simmer gently until thickened, for about 10 minutes.

4. Preheat oven to 375°F (190°C).

5. Remove ham from water, peel off the skin, and score the fat in a diamond pattern. Place the ham on a rack in a roasting pan, fat side up.

6. Brush with egg yolk, sprinkle with breadcrumbs if using.

7. Place it in a roasting pan. Stud with cloves, if desired, and baste with molasses glaze every 15-20 minutes. Bake for 45–60 minutes, until glossy and caramelized. Let rest 15 minutes before slicing. Serve warm.

VENISON STEW

They say Yorktown smelled of gunpowder and rot. But to the starving soldiers of 1781, it also smelled of venison—bubbling in iron pots stirred by women like Sarah Osborn Benjamin. She wore no uniform, held no rank—just a cloak, an apron, and a fire that never went out.

She followed the Continental Army with her husband, not only to Yorktown but through cold camps and endless marches. She fetched water, washed shirts stiff with blood and gun oil, and when the army dug in for its final siege, she cooked. *"We cooked and baked as fast as ever we could,"* she recalled later, *"and the meat was venison and beef, and the soldiers never seemed satisfied."*

She fed boys half her age who hadn't tasted real meat in weeks. She stirred while cannon thundered in the distance. And she watched victory rise over Virginia—only to watch, years later, as the memory of that victory left her behind. When the war ended, the women who served were forgotten. No medals. No pensions. Not even thanks.

Decades later, widowed and poor, Sarah sat before a Pennsylvania court to plead for a pension. She was in her eighties. Her hands trembled as she spoke, but her memory did not. She told of the campfires, the kettles, the smell of meat and smoke—and the hunger that never lifted.

This dish—venison roast or stew—is more than a recipe. It is a memorial to women's work in war: preserved in smoke and memory, stirred over fire, served without applause. The meat, she said, was a mix of venison and beef. And the soldiers never seemed satisfied.

Original Receipt

Lay a haunch of venison to the fire, baste with butter, and sprinkle with salt; when well soaked, flour it well, and keep basting till done. Serve with currant jelly or made gravy with wine and spices. Venison requires a brisk fire and constant basting, or it will dry and be spoiled. Venison can be roasted or adapted into a stew for bulk cooking.

VENNISON STEW (Continued)

<u>Modern Recipe</u>

Skill Level: Moderate
Prep Time: 25 minutes
Cook Time: 2½ - 3 hours
Total Time: About 3 hours
Yield: Serves 6 -8

Ingredients

- 1½ pounds venison, cubed stew meat
- 1½ pounds beef chuck, cubed
- 2 tbsp lard, butter, or oil
- 1 – 2 onions, chopped
- 3 carrots, sliced
- 2 – 3 parsnips or potatoes, cubes
- 1 bay leaf
- 1 tsp dried thyme
- ½ tsp ground allspice or clove (optional)
- salt and pepper to taste
- 3 cups beef broth
- 1 cup dry red wine or cider (or additional broth)
- 1 tbsp currant jelly or apple butter
- (Optional) 1 tbsp butter mixed with 1 tbsp flour

Directions

1. Heat fat in a heavy pot or Dutch oven over medium heat. Brown venison and beef in batches, seasoning lightly with salt and pepper.

2. Add chopped onions, carrots, and root vegetables. Sauté until softened. Stir in thyme, bay leaves, and optional spices.

3. Pour in wine or broth, scraping up browned bits from the pot. Add enough remaining liquid to cover the meat and bring to a simmer.

4. Cover and simmer gently for 2–3 hours, until the meat is tender and the stew has thickened to your desired consistency. Stir occasionally. Skim fat if needed.

5. Taste and adjust seasoning. Stir in currant jelly or cider reduction for a subtle colonial twist. Serve hot with coarse bread or johnnycakes for authenticity.

SEAFOOD

SEAFOOD

For the colonists living along the Atlantic seaboard, the rivers and bays were more than scenery—they were a lifeline. During the Revolution, when British blockades cut off trade and imported goods grew scarce, the sea became one of the surest sources of sustenance. Fish, shellfish, and river catches filled cooking pots from New England to the Carolinas, binding families to the tides as much as to the land.

Cod and haddock were the staples of New England, salted down in great barrels to last the year. "Salt fish" became so essential that it served as both ration and currency—feeding soldiers and sustaining commerce. Families boiled it with potatoes, baked it into pies, or stewed it with onions and pork fat into the hearty dish known as chowder. In wartime, chowder became more than a comfort food; it was a patriotic meal—simple, filling, and distinctly American.

Along the coast, clams and oysters were gathered in abundance. Oysters, once considered humble fare, became a daily source of nourishment for both families and soldiers. Tavern menus offered "oyster loaves"—bread hollowed out and filled with stewed oysters— while home kitchens simmered clam chowders or baked stuffed oysters with herbs. Lobsters, though plentiful, were still regarded as "poor man's food," fed to servants and prisoners long before they became a delicacy.

The sea was both pantry and provider, offering endurance when the land could not. From cod barrels and chowder pots to oyster loaves and shad feasts, the waters of the Atlantic helped carry the Revolution to victory—and left behind flavors that still endure on American tables today.

BROYLED LOBSTERS

In the 1770s, lobster was everywhere along New England's rocky shores. It washed up in piles after a storm, so abundant that many colonists considered it food for servants, apprentices, and prisoners. Indentured workers in Massachusetts even petitioned their masters, insisting they not be fed lobster more than three times a week—calling it a form of cruelty.

The scandal came when British officers in Boston turned the lowly lobster into a delicacy. At Loyalist suppers, red-coated gentlemen dined on lobster in cream sauce, while hungry Patriots looked on in anger. Pamphleteers seized the image: the bright red shell became a symbol of excess and oppression. It was no accident that British soldiers were derisively called "lobster backs." To the rebels, the color of the shell mirrored the uniforms of their occupiers—and serving lobster at a Loyalist table was seen as a quiet declaration of loyalty to the Crown.

So while farmers and soldiers ate lobster because it was cheap, those glittering dining rooms turned it into a statement of privilege. What one side called necessity, the other flaunted as luxury. And somewhere between the storm-tossed shore and the polished table, the humble lobster became a silent witness to revolution.

<u>Original Receipt</u>

"Take the taile of the lobsters and slitt them in two. Lay them on a gridiron and broyle them on a cleare fire till they are hott through, keeping them basting with butter. Then melt some butter and squeeze some juice of lemons in it. Serve with the sauce."
— 18th-Century New Jersey Recipes, National Park Service

<u>Modern Recipe</u>

Skill Level: Easy
Prep Time: 10 minutes
Cook Time: 10-12 minutes
Total Time: 25 minutes
Yield: Serves 2

BROYED LOBSTERS (Continued)

Ingredients

- 2 whole lobsters (about 1½ pounds each)
- ¼ cup butter, melted (plus more for basting)
- Juice of 1 lemon
- Pinch of salt

Directions

1. Preheat broiler or grill.
2. Split lobsters lengthwise. Clean.
3. Place the meat-side up on a broiler pan and brush it generously with melted butter.
4. Broil 15–20 minutes, basting occasionally with butter, until the meat is opaque and lightly browned on top.
5. Finish with a final drizzle of lemon juice and melted butter. Serve immediately.

CLAM CHOWDER

Clam chowder seems harmless—a steaming bowl of clams, onions, pork, and potatoes. But in Revolutionary America, food was never just food. It was identity, survival, and rebellion.

The first printed chowder recipe appeared in the *Boston Evening-Post* in 1751—written as a poem. Beyond nourishment, chowder became a way of life in New England, eaten at sea, in taverns, and around family tables. Sailors called it "chowda," swearing it kept them warm against the Atlantic wind.

For Boston's working families, chowder was a cheap one-pot meal: clams, pork scraps, and stale ship's biscuit simmered together into comfort. For Loyalists, the same dish was served with fine wine. Chowder crossed every boundary—rebels and royalists shared it, often within sight of each other, sometimes under the same roof.

Before the Revolution, New Englanders held lively "chowder parties" along the coast, cooking great kettles of it over open fires. Newspapers mocked them as noisy, boisterous, and drunk—but they were also democratic, gatherings where class and rank blurred in the steam.

Today, we carry on that tradition. We gather friends, raise a glass, and lift our spoons—continuing one of colonial America's most enduring customs. Chowder fed people at war and became, in its way, a symbol of fellowship: humble, hearty, and unmistakably New England.

CLAM CHOWDER (Continued)

<u>Original Receipt</u>

Boston Evening Post on September 23, 1751. Written as a poem in rhyming couplets, one of the quirkiest texts of the Revolution:

First lay some Onions to keep the Pork from burning.
Because in Chouder there can be no turning;
Then lay some Pork in Slices very thin,
This you in Chouder always must begin.

Next lay some Fish cut crosswise very nice,
Then season well with Pepper, Salt, and Spice;
Parsley, Sweet-Marjoram, Savory, and Thyme,
Then Biscuit next which must be soak'd some Time.

Thus your Foundation laid, you will be able,
To raise a Chouder, high as Tower of Babel;
For by repeating o'er the Same again,
You may make a Chouder for a thousand Men.

Last Bottle of Claret, with Water eno'
To smother them, you'll need a good Chouder.

Modern Recipe

Skill Level: Easy
Prep Time: 20 minutes
Cook Time: 35 - 40 minutes
Total Time: 1 hour
Yield: Serves 6

Ingredients

- 4 pounds littleneck clams

- 4 slices bacon, diced

- 1 onion, chopped

- 2 potatoes, cubed

- 2 cups heavy cream

- 2 tbsp butter

- Salt, black pepper, thyme

Directions

1. Steam the clams until they open. Remove the meat, chop coarsely, and reserve the cooking liquor.

2. Fry the bacon until crisp, then add the onion and cook until lightly browned.

3. Add potatoes, reserved liquor, and enough water to cover. Simmer until the potatoes are tender.

4. Stir in the chopped clams, cream, butter, and thyme. Season to taste and serve hot with oyster crackers or crusty bread.

CODFISH CAKES

Salt cod carried the Revolution. By the 1770s, Massachusetts fisheries produced more than 300,000 quintals of cod each year—nearly thirty million pounds—feeding not only New England, but also the Caribbean and Europe. Barrels of dried fish crowded Boston's wharves, traded for sugar, molasses, and hard currency that helped sustain the Patriot cause.

Patriot leaders understood its value. In Congress, John Adams called the New England fisheries "the nursery of seamen," essential to the survival of liberty itself. Cod was more than food; it was political power—a resource that tied the New England coast to the vast economy of the Atlantic world.

At Valley Forge in the bitter winter of 1777–78, supply records show that salt fish often replaced meat when livestock ran short. One weary officer admitted that the men grew "tired of the everlasting cod," tossing portions aside rather than eating. Yet for families at home, cod remained a lifeline. In Boston, widows and housewives stretched it with potatoes and onions into simple cakes that could feed many mouths at little cost.

In the kitchens of the enslaved, cod took on new forms—boiled, flaked, and folded into cornmeal to make sustaining stews and fritters. Its universality made it one of the few foods that crossed every line of the Revolution: from army camps to elite tables, from the wharves to the cabins. What was bitterness to a soldier in the snow was comfort to a mother feeding her children—proof that even the humblest ingredient could bind a nation together.

Original Receipt

Take good dry cod-fish, and having soaked it all night in fair water, changing the water once or twice to take away the salt, boil it tender. When it is cold, pick it very finely, removing all bones and skin.

Take an equal quantity of potatoes, well boiled and mashed smooth, and mix them with the cod-fish, adding a little butter if it is dry. Beat up one egg (or two if the quantity is large) and stir it well into the fish and potatoes. Season with a bit of pepper, and salt only if needful.

CODFISH CAKES (Continued)

Form the mixture into small cakes by hand, dredge them lightly with flour, and fry them in fresh butter till they are a fine brown on both sides. Serve them hot.

Modern Recipe

Skill Level: Easy
Prep Time: 20 minutes (plus soaking time if using salt cod)
Cook Time: 20 minutes
Total Time: About 40 minutes
Yield: Serves 4 - 6

Ingredients

- 1 pound salt cod (soaked overnight, water changed 2–3 times)
- or fresh cod, lightly salted
- 1 pound potatoes, boiled and mashed
- 1 egg, beaten
- 2 tbsp butter, melted
- 1–2 tbsp chopped parsley (optional but period-appropriate)
- freshly ground black pepper
- butter or oil, for frying
- lemon wedges, to serve

Directions:

1. If using salt cod, soak overnight, change the water several times. Boil until it is tender, drain, and flake finely.

2. Combine the cod with mashed potatoes, egg, butter, parsley, and black pepper. Mix until just blended.

3. Shape into small patties (about 3 inches wide) and chill 20–30 minutes to help them hold their shape.

4. Fry in butter over medium heat until golden brown on both sides.

5. Serve hot with lemon wedges on the side.

OYSTER STEW

In the great houses of Virginia, in kitchens where the fire never dimmed, enslaved African women stirred pots of milk, butter, and oysters—creating something unforgettable. What we call comfort food today was, in its beginning, the labor of the enslaved: prepared before dawn, carried to tables where they could not sit, praised in silence while their names went unspoken.

They had no cookbooks. They didn't need them. They carried recipes in memory and muscle—generations of flavor borne through bondage. In their hands, oyster stew became more than sustenance. It was refinement as defiance, mastery in a world that denied their humanity. They took what was cheap—oysters, milk, scraps of butter—and turned it into silk. They seasoned survival with salt and with quiet resistance.

The families who dined at those tables never knew the full recipe. They only knew it was good—too good to admit who made it. Like gumbo, jambalaya, and the fish fry, oyster stew did not descend from Europe's kitchens. It came from Africa—remembered across oceans, reshaped in bondage, rebuilt on American soil and sweat.

When we ladle it out today, oyster stew is not merely a dish of comfort. It is a record. A memory. A stolen recipe that endures—a testament to the genius and endurance of those whose hands fed a nation even as they hungered for freedom.

Original Receipt

Take a pint of oysters with their liquor, strain the liquor through a cloth and put it into a saucepan with the oysters. Add a bit of butter the size of a walnut, a spoonful of white wine, a little grated nutmeg and pepper. Stew them gently till they begin to curl. Serve hot with toasted sippets.

Modern Recipe

Skill Level: Easy
Prep Time: 10 minutes
Cook Time: 10 - 15 minutes
Total Time: 25 minutes
Yield: Serves 4

OYSTER STEW (Continued)

Ingredients

- 1 pint fresh oysters (with liquor)
- 2 tbsp unsalted butter
- ½ cup chopped celery (optional)
- 1 cup whole milk or half-and-half
- salt and pepper to taste
- pinch of nutmeg
- 1 tbsp dry sherry or white wine
- toasted baguette slices or crackers

Directions

1. In a saucepan, melt the butter and sauté the celery, if using, until softened.

2. Add oysters with their liquor and simmer gently until the edges begin to curl.

3. Stir in the milk, wine, and nutmeg. Warm gently, taking care not to let it boil.

4. Season to taste with salt and pepper. Serve hot with a toasted baguette or crackers.

CRAB FEAST

The rain came softly and suddenly—just enough to settle the dust, just enough to wake the ground. On the Virginia coast in the summer of 1777, a column of weary Hessian soldiers, hired by the British Crown, marched along the edge of enemy territory. Their boots were soaked. Their rations low. They were thousands of miles from home, and the war had long since stopped making sense.

And then the ground began to move. From small holes in the sand, tiny crabs scuttled out—red-legged, blue-shelled, twitching in the rain. *"We gathered and cooked an entire kettle full,"* one soldier wrote in his diary. *"They taste like ours."*

There were not many crabs, but they were warm. They tasted like home. The men boiled them in battered kettles over open fires, pulling the meat from the shells with blistered fingers. There were no recipes, no spices, no wine—just rain, fire, and crabs.

In the stillness after the meal, one soldier leaned back and said nothing. Later, he would write: *"For a moment, I forgot the longing, and the shot that missed my shoulder."*

Original Receipt

Take such crabs as you find by the riverbanks or shores, chiefly after rains, when they emerge from holes in the sand. Clean them of soil and gather enough for the pot.

Place over flame a kettle with fresh water and add a pinch of salt if at hand. Boil the crabs till they turn red, and the shells crack. If herbs or onions are available, add them for taste, else serve plain.

Take bread if there is any and give thanks for a hot meal.

Modern Recipe

Skill Level: Easy
Prep Time: 10 minutes
Cook Time: 15 minutes
Total Time: 25 minutes
Yield: Serves 4

CRAB FEAST (Continued)

Ingredients

- 2 pounds blue crabs, cleaned (or use small crabs or soft shells if available)

- 1 tbsp sea salt

- 1 tbsp black peppercorn (optional)

- 1 bay leaf (optional but period-appropriate)

- water to cover

- Optional: 1 chopped onion or wild greens (e.g., parsley, ramps)

Directions

1. Clean the crabs: Rinse them thoroughly in cold water.

2. Fill a pot: Add water to a large pot that is just enough to cover the crabs. Add salt, bay leaf, and pepper if using.

3. Boil: Bring to a full rolling boil. Add the crabs carefully. Cover and boil until the mixture turns bright red (about 10–15 minutes).

4. Serve: Drain and serve hot. Eat with fingers: no butter, no lemons, just crab, water, and maybe coarse bread.

TAVERN FARE

TAVERN FARE

During the Revolution, taverns were more than places to drink—they were the heart of colonial life. Every town and village had one, marked by a painted sign swinging above the road. Within those dimly lit rooms, men gathered to argue politics, trade news, and plot rebellion. Taverns served as post offices, meeting halls, and courtrooms; even the Boston Tea Party was first imagined in the smoke-filled corners of a tavern room.

The food was plain, hearty, and meant to fill bellies fast. Travelers could expect bread and cheese, salted meats, or a meat pie waiting beneath a thick crust of pastry. Stews of beef, mutton, or pork simmered in heavy kettles, stretched with onions, carrots, and potatoes. Chowders rich with fish, pork fat, and hardtack were staples in New England, while in the South, taverns served corn mush, fried catfish, or ham with greens. Plates were often flanked by pickled vegetables, vinegar for seasoning, and dense rye or "Indian" bread made from cornmeal.

Dessert was rare and simple: gingerbread, apple pie, or a pudding of stale bread sweetened with molasses. More often, tavern keepers served sweetened drinks instead—ale, rum punch, or "flip," that fiery mixture of beer, rum, and molasses frothed with a red-hot iron. These drinks kept the rooms noisy long after the meal was gone.

What tavern food lacked in elegance, it made up for in comfort and camaraderie. In the years of the Revolution, taverns fed more than bodies. They fed ideas, courage, and the spirit of independence itself.

And so, in these rooms warmed by firelights and argument, history was carried forward not only by speeches and signatures, but by shared meals. A trencher of stew passed across a table, a loaf broken in two, a mug raised in weary fellowship—these were the small, human moments that sustained a people in uncertain times. Long after the candles burned low and the benches were stacked against the wall, the tavern remained in memory as a place where ordinary men and women found strength in one another. In feeding the hungry traveler and the restless patriot alike, taverns became unlikely kitchens of revolution, where the future of a nation was nourished one simple dish at a time.

JAMES HEMINGS' MACARONI AND CHEESE

Lanterns flickered in Virginia's taverns, casting long shadows over bowls of stew, salted pork, and coarse bread—the ordinary fare of common tables. But at Monticello, where Thomas Jefferson dined with diplomats and dignitaries, another dish often appeared: macaroni baked beneath a golden crust of cheese.

Macaroni was a curiosity imported from Europe, a delicacy Jefferson first encountered during his travels in France and Italy. He returned to Virginia with both the pasta and the instructions to prepare it, entrusting the task to his French-trained enslaved chef, James Hemings. In the kitchens of Monticello, Hemings mastered the dish— tender macaroni layered with butter and cheese, baked until bubbling and bronzed.

The result was a union of Old-World elegance and New World invention, a recipe that reflected Jefferson's cosmopolitan taste and Hemings's extraordinary skill. It stood in sharp contrast to the rustic stews and salted meats of the tavern table. Out of that contrast— between privilege and labor, refinement and bondage became a dish that would one day belong to everyone.

From those beginnings, macaroni and cheese traveled far beyond Monticello's hilltop, passing from mansion kitchens to family tables across the nation. What began as the food of diplomats became, in time, the taste of home—a comfort born of complexity, and a legacy shared by all.

Original Receipt

Take macaroni, and boil it in water till tender, but not broken. Drain it well. Lay it in a dish with butter, and grate cheese over it, with a bit of pepper. Add more macaroni, butter, and cheese till the dish is full, finishing with cheese on top. Put it into a Dutch oven, or before the fire, and let it stand till it is well heated through, and the cheese is melted and lightly browned. Serve hot.

Modern Recipe

Skill Level: Moderate
Prep Time: 20 minutes
Cook Time: 25 minutes
Total Time: 45 minutes
Yield: Serves 4 - 6

JAMES HEMINGS' MACARONI AND CHEESE (Continued)

Ingredients

- 8 oz macaroni (elbow or tube)
- 3 tbsp butter
- 1 cup whole milk (warm)
- 1½ cups grated cheese:
    - ¾ cup Parmesan or aged Gruyère
    - ¾ cup sharp white cheddar (for richness and familiarity)
- Freshly ground black pepper
- Salt, to taste
- Optional (but recommended): a pinch of nutmeg
- Optional topping: ¼ cup fine breadcrumbs mixed with 1 tbsp melted butter

Directions

1. Boil the macaroni in salted water until just tender; drain well.
2. In a saucepan over low heat, melt the butter. Add the warm milk and stir gently.
3. Add the cheeses gradually, stirring until smooth and melted. Do not let the mixture boil.
4. Season with black pepper, a small pinch of nutmeg, and salt only if needed.
5. Fold in the macaroni and transfer to a buttered baking dish.
6. Top lightly with buttered breadcrumbs if using.
7. Bake at 375°F (190°C) for 20–25 minutes, until bubbling and lightly browned.
8. Let rest 5 minutes before serving.

Cook's Note: *James Hemings was trained in French cuisine while enslaved by Thomas Jefferson. He negotiated his freedom in 1796, the first American to bring classical French cookery to the new republic.*

BOSTON BAKED BEANS

In the tavern hearth, a Dutch oven sat half-buried in coals, its lid rattling with the slow bubble of beans, salt pork, and molasses. The smell was thick—earthy and sweet—filling every corner of the room. For weary travelers and off-duty militiamen, a steaming bowl of baked beans was both comfort and endurance: filling, inexpensive, and built to last.

One Massachusetts soldier, Joseph Plumb Martin, later remembered the plain diet of the army and how beans often stood between the troops and hunger. *"Our rations were sometimes scant,"* he wrote, *"but beans were ever a friend in want, filling us better than the bread."* Soldiers carried small sacks of beans in their knapsacks; when boiled over smoky campfires, they became the difference between weakness and strength.

Back in Boston, Puritan custom-made beans a weekly ritual. On Saturday nights, tavern keepers and housewives slid their bean pots into brick ovens, where they baked slowly until Sunday dinner was served. In crowded taverns, bowls of beans passed from hand to hand as men argued politics, traded news of battles, and pledged their loyalty to the Patriot cause.

But beans carried more than flavor; they carried a story. The molasses that sweetened them came from Caribbean trade routes, bound up with the brutal economy of the Atlantic world. The beans themselves were native to New England soil—humble, sustaining, and deeply American.

It was said that a man could march a day on beans alone. And in a Revolution built on endurance, that was no small gift.

Original Receipt

Take white beans, pick and wash them, and soak them all night in cold water. In the morning, boil them in fresh water until they begin to soften but are not yet broken.

Take salt pork, and score the rind. Put a piece of it in the bottom of an earthen pot or Dutch oven, then add the beans, with an onion stuck with a few cuts, if it be liked. Mix molasses and a little mustard with hot water, and pour it over the beans till they are just covered. Add salt only if needful; the pork is already salted.

BOSTON BAKED BEANS (Continued)

Cover the pot close, and set it in a slow oven, or bury it near the hearth embers, to bake gently for five or six hours, keeping it from drying, and adding a little hot water if required. When well browned and thick, serve hot.

Modern Recipe

Skill Level: Moderate
Prep Time: 15 minutes (plus soaking overnight)
Cook Time: 5 – 6 hours
Total Time: About 6½
Yield: Serves 6 -8

Ingredients:

- 2 cups dried navy beans
- ½ lb. salt pork or thick bacon
- ⅓ cup molasses
- 1 tbsp brown sugar
- 1 tsp mustard powder
- 1 small onion, chopped
- Salt, to taste

Directions

1. Soak beans overnight. Drain.
2. Simmer beans in fresh water until tender but not falling apart.
3. Layer beans, pork, and onion in a Dutch oven.
4. Mix molasses, sugar, and mustard with 1 cup of hot water; then pour it over the beans.
5. Cover and bake at 275°F for 5–6 hours, checking occasionally and adding a little water if the mixture becomes too thick.

Cook's Note: *In colonial Boston, baked beans were traditionally left in brick ovens overnight, warming taverns and homes until Sunday morning. The sweet-salty aroma became a New England signature, both a Sabbath meal and a symbol of thrift.*

VIRGINA HAM BISCUITS

The tavern hearth glowed with steady heat, the air thick with woodsmoke, cider, and the scent of fresh biscuits rising in iron pans. A cook's hands moved quickly rolling dough, cutting rounds, slipping them into the oven. Within minutes, the golden biscuits were split and filled with thin slices of salt-cured Virginia ham, smoky and sharp. Simple, portable, and deeply satisfying, they were the taste every traveler longed for.

George Washington himself often paused at Williamsburg's Christiana Campbell's Tavern, where Virginia's famed hams were served with pride. To Washington and his fellow officers, those biscuits carried more than flavor—they carried memory, a reminder of home amid the hardships of war. Smokehouse ham was Virginia's signature gift, a symbol of endurance from a land balanced between struggle and hope.

For weary Continentals, a ham biscuit pressed into their hands by a kindly tavern keeper was more than a meal—it was an act of quiet patriotism. As one officer later recalled, *"The country people would not let us go hungry—ham and bread they gave freely, and it cheered us on our way."*

In the noisy warmth of the tavern, as mugs of cider clinked and voices rose in talk of liberty, the humble ham biscuit became something greater than food. It was Virginia's welcome to soldier and statesman alike—a small, flaky pledge that the Revolution was sustained not only on battlefields, but at the hearths and tables of ordinary people.

Original Receipt

Take fine flour, and mix therein a little salt. Rub in butter or lard till it be like crumbs. Wet it with sour milk, or milk turned with a little vinegar, and make it into a soft paste.

Roll it out lightly, and cut it into small rounds. Take cured Virginia ham cut very small, and lay a little upon each, folding the paste over, or pressing it within the biscuit. Lay them upon a baking sheet, and bake them in a quick oven till they rise and are lightly browned. Serve hot.

VIRGINIA HAM BISCUITS (Continued)

Modern Recipe

Skill Level: Easy
Prep Time: 15 minutes
Cook Time: 15 minutes
Total Time: 30 minutes
Yield: Serves 12 biscuits

Ingredients:

- 2 cups of all-purpose flour

- 1 tbsp baking powder

- ½ tsp salt

- ½ cup cold butter, diced

- ¾ cup milk (or buttermilk or whole milk)

- ½ cup finely diced cured Virginia ham

Directions

1. Heat oven to 400°F (200°C).

2. In a bowl, whisk flour, baking powder, and salt.

3. Cut in butter until mixture resembles coarse crumbs.

4. Stir in ham and buttermilk just until the dough comes together.

5. Roll to ½-inch thickness, cut rounds, and place on a baking sheet.

6. Bake for 12–15 minutes, or until golden. Serve warm.

Cook's Note*: In colonial taverns, ham biscuits were often served alongside mugs of cider or small beer. Travelers tucked them into coat pockets for the road—a portable comfort and a taste of Virginia's famed hospitality.*

MEAT PIE

When British troops occupied New York from 1776 to 1778, the city's taverns became contested ground. For Patriots, they were secret meeting houses—alive with whispered plots and coded toasts. For British officers, they were extensions of the officer's mess, places to dine, drink, and display refinement amid war.

Fraunces Tavern, still standing today, hosted both kinds of guests. Under Sir William Howe's command, his officers filled their tables with imported wines, fine cheeses, and meat pies—pastries stuffed with beef, veal, or mutton, seasoned with pepper and cloves. While ordinary soldiers made do with beans, salt pork, and hard bread, Howe's staff enjoyed suppers that tasted of London. Patriots mocked this indulgence, pointing to the contrast between soldiers' fare and aristocratic excess.

For tavern keepers, the meat pie was both business and theater—a dish that could be baked in advance, sliced and served hot, hearty enough for a hungry officer yet polished enough for His Majesty's table. In occupied New York, a steaming pie was more than food; it was a symbol of the gulf that defined the war itself: between rulers and rebels, luxury and scarcity, power and the will to endure.

Note: Minced Pie and Meat Pie in Colonial America were not the same dish. **Key Difference:**

- *Minced Pie* = festive, spiced, with fruit (holiday, genteel tables).

- *Meat Pie* = everyday tavern fare, plain savory filling (common suppers, officer's mess).

Original Receipt

Take beef, veal, or mutton, and mince it small. Finely chop an onion and mix it with the meat. Season it with pepper and a little nutmeg or cloves, if you like. Add small bits of suet or butter, and a spoonful or two of good broth, if the meat is lean.

Make a paste of flour, butter or lard, a little salt, and water, and work it well. Line a dish with the paste, put in the meat, and cover it with a lid of paste. Cut a hole in the top.

Bake it in a quick oven till the crust is well colored, and the meat thoroughly done. Serve hot.

MEAT PIE (Continued)

Modern Recipe

Skill Level: Moderate

Prep Time: 25 minutes

Cook Time: 45 minutes

Total Time: 1 hour 10 minutes

Yield: Serves 1 (9-inch) pie

Ingredients:

- ¾ pound ground beef
- ¾ pound ground pork (or veal)
- 1 medium onion, very finely chopped
- 2 tbsp butter
- ½ tsp ground nutmeg
- ¼ tsp ground cloves (or allspice)
- ½ tsp black pepper
- 1 tsp salt
- ¼ cup beef broth (or milk)
- 1 tbsp flour (binder)
- 2 prepared pie crusts

Directions

1. Heat oven to 375°F (190°C).
2. Melt butter in a skillet; sauté onion until soft, not browned.
3. Add beef and pork: cook over medium heat just until no longer pink, breaking up the meat as it browns.
4. Stir in spices, salt, pepper, flour, and broth; remove from heat.
5. Spoon the filling into the bottom crust, cover with the top crust, seal the edges, and cut vents.

6. Bake 40–45 minutes, until the crust is deeply golden and the filling is bubbling at the edges.

7. Rest 10 minutes before slicing.

Cook's Note: *In colonial taverns, meat pies were sold by the slice—a hearty, portable meal served hot from the hearth. Officers' pies were spiced and refined, while standard versions were plain but filling.*

PYE OF FOWL
(CHICKEN POT PIE)

When Sir Henry Clinton replaced Sir William Howe as commander in 1778, New York was already a city of divided loyalties and whispered scandal. Clinton lacked the charm of his predecessor. Patriots mocked him as plodding, jealous, and forever grumbling about shortages. Yet under occupation, the city's taverns still glowed with candlelight—their back rooms alive with Loyalist toasts, clandestine bargains, and Patriot spies listening through the smoke.

Clinton's officers demanded refinement even in war. At Fraunces Tavern, platters of roast, imported wine, and steaming "pye of fowl" were set before them—tender chicken stewed with onions, cream, and spices, sealed beneath a golden crust. It was meant to conjure London's comfort, a fleeting taste of home. But to Patriots watching from the shadows, those suppers stood as symbols of indulgence—luxury in the midst of want, while Continental soldiers starved on hard bread and thin broth.

Rumors swirled that Clinton himself, brooding over his post, passed his evenings in such taverns, where secrets traded hands as easily as coin. Spies slipped notes across ale mugs; couriers met under the hum of music and laughter. Some whispered that seduction had become a weapon of war—Loyalist hostesses charming, red-coated officers while quietly feeding intelligence to both sides.

In that world, the chicken pie—rich and steaming in its crust—became more than a meal. In Clinton's New York, it was the centerpiece of power and intrigue, served at tables where alliances shifted, and the war for hearts and loyalties was fought one course at a time.

Original Receipt

(Take a fowl and cut it into joints. Season it with pepper and a little salt and lay it in a dish. Put it a little butter, and if it be liked, a few slices of onion. Pour in some good broth, enough to moisten it, but not to overflow the paste. Make a paste with flour and butter or suet, and a little salt, wet with water. Line the dish with paste, put in the fowl, and cover it with a lid of paste. Cut a hole in the top. Bake it in a quick oven till the crust is well coloured, and the fowl tender. Serve hot.

PYE OF FOWL (CHICKEN POT PIE) (Continued)

<u>Modern Recipe</u>

Skill Level: Moderate
Prep Time: 25 minutes
Cook Time: 45 minutes
Total Time: 1 hour 10 minutes
Yield: Serves 1 (9-inch) pie

Ingredients

- $1\frac{1}{2}$ pounds chicken thighs, cut into bite-sized pieces
- 2 tbsp butter
- 1 onion, finely diced
- 2 carrots, diced
- 2 celery stalks, diced
- 2 tbsp flour
- 2 cups chicken stock
- $\frac{1}{2}$ cup heavy cream
- 1 egg yolk
- 1 tsp salt
- $\frac{1}{2}$ tsp black pepper
- Optional but highly recommended:
- 1 tsp fresh thyme (or $\frac{1}{2}$ tsp dried)
- 1 tsp lemon juice (or a splash of dry sherry)
- 2 pie crusts (or puff pastry)

Directions

1. Preheat oven to 375°F (190°C).
2. In a large skillet, melt butter over medium heat. Add onion, carrots, and celery; cook until softened but not browned.
3. Stir in flour; cook 1 minute.
4. Gradually add stock, simmer until thickened.

PYE OF FOWL (CHICKEN POT PIE) (Continued)

5. Add chicken and cook just until opaque on the outside.

6. Whisk cream and egg yolk together. This step enriches the filling, giving it a velvety texture. Remove the skillet from the heat and stir the mixture gently.

7. Season with salt, pepper, thyme, and lemon (or sherry).

8. Spoon the mixture into the bottom crust, cover with the top crust, seal edges, and cut vents.

9. Bake 40–50 minutes, until the crust is golden and the filling is bubbling.

10. Rest 10 minutes before serving.

Cook's Note: *In colonial taverns, "Pye of Fowl" could be made with chicken, duck, or pigeon. The crusts were often heavy and meant to preserve the filling for days of practical luxury in uncertain times.*

DESSERTS & SWEETS

DESSERTS AND SWEETS

Dessert in the eighteenth century was more than the final course of a meal, it was a symbol of status, celebration, and, during the Revolution, resilience. Colonial Americans did not eat sweets every day; sugar, spices, and dried fruits were costly imports. Yet on holidays, in taverns, and in the homes of the wealthy, desserts were treated as occasions of extravagance.

The most beloved colonial sweets came from English tradition: plum puddings heavy with suet and dried fruit, steamed for hours on Christmas Day; mince pies filled with spiced meat, raisins, and brandy at New Year's; and in genteel parlors, syllabubs—frothy mixtures of cream and wine—served in delicate glasses beside trifles of sponge, custard, and fruit. Such dishes were as much for display as for taste, gestures of refinement in a young society eager to prove its cultivation.

But the Revolution changed the table. British blockades cut off access to imported sugar and dried fruit, forcing colonists to improvise. Patriots turned to maple sugar, honey, and molasses, crafting sweets that were simpler, humbler, and distinctly American. Indian pudding— a slow-baked custard of cornmeal, milk, and molasses—became a patriotic dish, celebrating native ingredients over British wheat. Gingerbread, too, was cherished in homes and army camps alike: fragrant, durable, easily shared.

Even desserts could be political. Tea was boycotted, but households proudly brewed "Liberty teas" from local herbs to serve beside their cakes. Large Election Cakes, studded with raisins and spice, fed crowds gathered for militia musters and voting days—blending civic duty with celebration.

By war's end, the taste of sweetness had come to mean more than luxury. It was a mark of endurance—of a people who had learned to make do, and in the process, to make something entirely their own.

DOLLEY'S GINGERBREAD

In the crowded parlors of the early White House, Dolley Madison was more than a hostess—she reigned. Her Wednesday-night receptions, fondly called "squeezes," drew hundreds of guests into candlelit rooms thick with perfume, politics, and the scent of gingerbread warm from the hearth. There were no velvet ropes or stiff protocols. Senators mingled with society wives. French diplomats gossiped over punch. Through it all, Dolley moved with practiced ease, offering cake and conversation in equal measure, her presence making clear—without a word spoken—that she understood the power of the room.

Her critics called her "Queen Dolley." She did not object. She believed that hospitality could steady tempers and soften hardened opinions, and she wielded it skillfully. One rival complained that the President's house had become "a bakehouse of democratic mischief." Others whispered that she exercised more influence than President Madison himself—and did so not through speeches or decrees, but through warmth, charm, and the quiet ritual of shared food.

When the British entered Washington in 1814, Dolley made history by ensuring the rescue of George Washington's portrait and safeguarding treasured household silver before fleeing the burning city. Later tradition would also place her beloved gingerbread among the comforts she refused to abandon. Whether fact or memory, the story endures because it captures something true: Dolley understood that diplomacy could be served with sugar as well as steel.

Dolley Madison mastered the politics of pleasure. With wit, warmth, and an unerring instinct for people, she transformed the nation's capital from a provincial town into a social stage—and presided over it, smiling, from behind a tray of gingerbread.

<u>Original Receipt</u>

One pound of flour, one pound of sugar, one pound of butter, four eggs, one gill of cream, one gill of milk, one ounce of ginger, a little cinnamon, one spoonful of rose-water; knead stiff, roll thin, cut into shapes, bake quick.

DOLLEY'S GINGERBREAD (Continued)

Modern Recipe

Skill Level: Easy
Prep Time: 20 minutes
Cook Time: 40 minutes
Total Time: 1 hour
Yield: Serves 1 (8 X 8 inch)

Ingredients

- 2 cups of all-purpose flour

- 1 tsp baking soda

- ½ tsp salt

- 1 tsp ground ginger

- 1 tsp cinnamon

- ½ tsp nutmeg

- ½ cup unsalted butter, softened

- ½ cup brown sugar

- 1 egg

- ¾ cup unsulphured molasses

- ¾ cup hot water

- Zest of 1 orange

- Powdered sugar or molasses glaze for topping

Directions

1. Preheat oven to 350°F. Grease or line an 8×8" pan.

2. In a medium bowl, whisk together flour, baking soda, salt, and spices.

3. In another bowl, cream butter and sugar. Beat in egg.

4. Stir in molasses, orange zest, and hot water.

DOLLEY'S GINGERBREAD (Continued)

5. Add the dry ingredients to the wet mixture and stir until smooth. Pour it into the pan.

6. Bake for 35–40 minutes, or until the center springs back when lightly touched.

7. Cool. Dust with powdered sugar or glaze. Serve with tea and gossip.

Cook's Note: *The recipe echoes early American versions flavored with molasses rather than treacle. The addition of orange zest was a later refinement, reflecting the influence of Dolley's sophisticated palate and imported citrus in Washington's market.*

POUND CAKE

Pound cake was never just cake. To British generals in America, it was a taste of home—dense with sugar, eggs, and butter, perfumed with Madeira wine and rosewater. It was a dessert of refinement, eaten with silver forks from porcelain plates. But in the years of revolution, that refinement became scandal.

The British had displayed their taste for indulgence before—most famously at the Mischianza Ball in Philadelphia in 1778. While Washington's men starved at Valley Forge, red-coated officers and Loyalist ladies feasted beneath chandeliers on frosted cakes and sugared fruits. Patriots mocked the spectacle as proof that Britain's leaders cared more for trifles than for victory.

Three years later, at Yorktown, the contrast turned tragic. As French and American cannon pounded the British lines, General Charles Cornwallis's officers still dined with ceremony—silver polished, claret poured, slices of Madeira-soaked pound cake set out as if the empire itself were not collapsing outside their tents. Eyewitnesses remembered the music and the feasting continuing even into the siege's final nights. Officers dined like gentlemen while their soldiers went hungry.

On October 19, 1781, Cornwallis surrendered—refusing to appear in person, sending his deputy instead. A Patriot pamphlet later sneered: *"There was cake and claret. Ours was crust and courage."*

Pound cake, once a symbol of elegance, became a metaphor for Britain's undoing—sweetness amid ruin, feasting in the shadow of defeat, the taste of an empire crumbling, one sugared slice at a time.

Original Receipt

Take one pound of sifted flour, one pound of powdered loaf sugar, and one pound of fresh butter. Beat the butter to a cream, then beat in the sugar. Beat ten eggs very light and stir them gradually into the butter and sugar; then add by degrees the flour, a glass of wine, and some rose-water. Bake in a moderate oven.

POUND CAKE (Continued)

Modern Recipe

Skill Level: Easy
Prep Time: 20 minutes
Cook Time: 55 minutes
Total Time: 1 hour 15 minutes
Yield: Serves 1 loaf or bundt cake

Ingredients

- 1 cup (2 sticks) unsalted butter, softened
- 1½ cups of sugar
- 4 large eggs
- 2 cups of all-purpose flour
- ½ tsp salt
- 1 tsp vanilla extract or 1 Tbsp rosewater
- 3 Tbsp Madeira wine or sherry
- zest of 1 lemon

Directions

1. Preheat oven to 350°F. Grease a loaf or bundt pan.

2. In a large bowl, cream butter and sugar together until pale and fluffy. Beat in eggs one at a time.

3. Fold in flour and salt in two additions, mixing only until just combined to avoid toughness.

4. Stir in vanilla/rosewater, Madeira, and lemon zest.

5. Pour into pan. Bake until well risen and richly golden, about 50–60 minutes.

6. Cool before slicing. Serve with scandal.

7. *Optional:* Brush the warm cake with a little Madeira or simple syrup for a glossy finish—a touch of Loyalist luxury.

POUND CAKE (Continued)

Cook's Note: *Madeira wine, a favorite of British officers, was imported through colonial trade networks until the Revolution disrupted supply. Pound cakes flavored with it became a symbol of refined taste — and, later, of excess.*

Illustration: Colonial-style pound cake, c. 1775.

SHREWSBURY CAKES

In June of 1778, Philadelphia was a city caught between celebration and uncertainty. The British had just withdrawn after months of occupation, leaving behind a battered but unbowed capital. As Washington's troops marched through in pursuit of the retreating redcoats, life began, slowly, to stitch itself back together. Amid the lingering scent of gunpowder and the clatter of departing armies, Philadelphians returned to their parlors, churches, and hearths— determined to reclaim the rhythms of ordinary life.

It was in this atmosphere that weddings resumed. Ann Willing Bingham—celebrated as one of the most dazzling women of Revolutionary Philadelphia—was the wife of William Bingham, among the richest men in the new nation. Renowned for her beauty, wit, and influence, she became a leading hostess of the Republic's early years. Supplies were scarce, luxury goods looted or hoarded, but brides and their families improvised with grace and pride. At tables laid with linen and candlelight, Shrewsbury Cakes often appeared—small, buttery biscuits scented with nutmeg or caraway. They were simple enough to bake with strained ingredients, yet elegant enough to honor the day.

The cakes themselves were old favorites, brought from England, baked for weddings and feasts since the Tudor age. But on the cobbled streets of post-occupation Philadelphia, their meaning changed. For Patriot families, serving Shrewsbury Cakes in 1778 was an act of quiet transformation—turning a genteel English custom into an American one.

What had once been a token of loyalty to the crown became, in that fragile moment, a declaration of independence by other means: the taste of continuity reclaimed, and of people learning to celebrate in their own way.

Original Receipt

Shrewsbury Cakes. One pound of butter, three-quarters of a pound of sugar, a little mace, four eggs, one pound and a quarter of flour; roll thin, cut, and bake quick.

SHREWSBURRY CAKES (Continued)

Modern Recipe

Skill Level: Easy
Prep Time: 15minutes
Cook Time: 10- 12 minutes
Total Time: 25 minutes
Yield: Serves 2 dozen small cakes

Ingredients

- 1 cup (2 sticks) unsalted butter, softened
- ¾ cup sugar
- 2 egg yolks
- 2 cups of All-Purpose flour
- ½ tsp ground mace or nutmeg (mace is more traditional)
- Pinch of salt
- 1 tsp vanilla extract(optional)

Directions

1. Preheat oven to 350°F. Line a baking sheet with parchment.
2. Cream butter and sugar until light. Beat in egg yolks.
3. Mix in flour, mace, and salt until dough forms.
4. Roll dough to ¼-inch thickness. Cut into rounds or simple shapes.
5. Bake 10–12 minutes, until golden at the edges.
6. Serve warm—with coffee, cider, or rebellion.

PEGGY SHIPPEN'S SYLLABUB "SECRET" RECEIPT

Philadelphia glittered under British occupation in the winter of 1778. While soldiers drilled in the streets and ordinary families struggled to find flour, the grand homes of Loyalist families still resounded with music, laughter, and the scent of sweet things. None shone brighter than the townhouse of Margaret "Peggy" Shippen—the beautiful young daughter of a wealthy judge.

Barely eighteen, Peggy was whispered about across the city. British officers called her enchanting. The Patriots called her dangerous. She seemed to thrive on both reputations. Raised in privilege and accustomed to entertaining, Peggy moved easily through candlelit parlors where crystal glasses caught the light and fashionable desserts signaled refinement as clearly as silk gowns or powdered hair.

At one such gathering, tables gleamed with jellies, candied fruits, and syllabub—a frothy confection of cream, sugar, wine, and lemon, served chilled in delicate glasses. Light, fashionable, and best prepared fresh, syllabub was a staple of genteel tables in both England and the American colonies, particularly in households with access to fresh dairy and imported sugar.

It was within these glittering Loyalist circles that Peggy crossed paths with Major John André, the British officer and amateur poet. Whether their exchanges were flirtation or merely polite wit remains unknown, but their worlds undeniably overlapped in drawing rooms where conversation flowed as freely as wine.

In hindsight, the syllabub served at Peggy Shippen's table seems more than a simple indulgence. Light, intoxicating, and deceptively sweet, it mirrored the social world she inhabited—one where charm could mask allegiance and where private conversations might quietly alter the course of history. Within two years, Peggy would marry General Benedict Arnold, and together they would nearly hand West Point to the British Crown.

PEGGY SHIPPENS SYLLABUB "SECRET" RECEIPT (Continued)

<u>Original Receipt</u>

To make a fine Syllabub from the Cow. Sweeten a quart of cider with double-refined sugar, grate in the rind of a lemon, add the juice, then milk your cow into it. As the froth rises, take it off with a spoon into your syllabub glasses or pots, and continue until you have filled them. They will keep well for a week.

<u>Modern Recipe</u>

Skill Level: Easy
Prep Time: 15 minutes - including whisking and mixing.
Chill Time: 1 hour
Total Time: 1 hour 15 minutes
Yield: Serves 4

Ingredients

- 1 cup heavy cream

- ½ cup sweet white wine (or hard cider for authenticity)

- ¼ cup sugar

- Zest and juice of ½ lemon

- Optional: freshly grated nutmeg for garnish

Directions

1. In a mixing bowl, combine the wine (or cider), lemon juice, zest, and sugar.

2. Stir until the sugar dissolves.

3. In a separate chilled bowl, whip the cream until soft peaks form.

4. Gently fold the wine mixture into the whipped cream until smooth and lightly aerated.

5. Spoon into small glass cups or dessert bowls.

6. Chill for at least 1 hour before serving.

7. Sprinkle lightly with nutmeg before serving.

Cook's Note: *In the 18th century, syllabub was both a drink and a dessert—served freshly whipped or allowed to separate into creamy layers above wine.*

COLONIAL DONUTS

In colonial New England, Muster Days were part drill, part festival. By law, able-bodied men were required to gather several times each year to train with the local militia. The fields rang with musket fire and shouted commands, but they also filled with families, neighbors, and vendors who turned the day into a communal celebration.

Food was central to the occasion. Women fried up batches of what they called "dough nuts"—small balls of sweetened dough, spiced with nutmeg or cinnamon, dropped into hot lard until golden and dusted with sugar. Alongside barrels of cider and trays of gingerbread, platters of doughnuts waited for the men who had drilled and the families who had come to watch.

Muster Days were as political as they were festive. Leaders like John Hancock and Samuel Adams often appeared, using the gatherings to speak of liberty and the need for vigilance. In those moments, even a humble fried cake carried meaning: it was the food of the people, shared as ordinary colonists readied themselves to defend their rights.

Though the modern spelling "doughnut" would come later, the colonial version—crisp, fragrant, and sweet—was already beloved. To bite into one on Muster Day was to taste both fellowship and resolve: a small comfort served in the shadow of revolution.

Original Receipt

Make a light dough with flour, milk, and a little yeast, knead well, and when risen, cut into pieces the bigness of a walnut; fry them in hog's lard, and when done, dust with sugar.

Modern Recipe

Skill Level: Moderate
Prep Time: 20 minutes
Cook Time: 10 minutes
Total Time: 30 minutes
Yield: Serves 10 – 12 donuts

Ingredients

- 2 ½ cups all-purpose flour
- 2 tsp baking powder

COLONIAL DONUTS (Continued)

- ½ tsp salt
- ½ tsp nutmeg or cinnamon
- ½ cup sugar
- 2 eggs
- ½ cup milk
- 3 tbsp melted butter
- neutral oil or lard for frying
- powdered sugar or cinnamon-sugar for dusting

Directions

1. In a large bowl, whisk together the flour, baking powder, salt, nutmeg, and sugar.

2. In another bowl, beat the eggs with the milk and melted butter.

3. Stir the wet ingredients into the dry until a soft dough forms.

4. Roll out on a floured surface to about ½ inch thick. Cut into rounds, with or without a center hole.

5. Heat lard or oil to 350°F (175°C). Fry the doughnuts 2–3 minutes per side, until puffed and golden.

6. Drain on paper towels and dust generously with powdered sugar or cinnamon sugar.

7. Serve warm.

Cook's Note: *Early doughnuts were often fried in rendered hog's lard and flavored with nutmeg or mace. The hole in the center appeared later in the 19th century—colonial "doughnuts" were typically small, round cakes fried whole.*

BEVERAGES

BEVERAGES

"Drink, that we may remember."

Long before ice cubes clinked in cocktail glasses or lemon slices floated in fizzy water, the people of early America gathered around tankards, flagons, and steaming mugs to find warmth, cheer, and a brief escape from the hardships of life. Whether in a bustling port tavern, a snow-dusted farmhouse, or a candlelit drawing room, drink was both necessity and ceremony—strong or subtle, spirited or sweet, and always central to the colonial table.

To modern eyes, the line between beverage and medicine may seem blurred. To the eighteenth-century mind, it was perfectly clear. If it was brewed for pleasure, it was a beverage; if it was boiled, steeped, or fortified for healing, it belonged in the apothecary's chest. That is why all mulled wines, punches, ciders, and cordials belong here—and not among the cough syrups and tonics. This section is for toasts, not treatments.

In the colonies, taverns were temples, and drinking was more than refreshment; it was ritual. Rum punch passed after battles. Madeira graced the table of every patriot-turned-president. Even switchel—a sharp mix of vinegar, ginger, and molasses—was poured by the gallon in hayfields and harvest barns. They drank to survive. They drank to remember. They drank to belong.

So raise a mug to their memory—and mind your P's and Q's.

A Proper Colonial Toast

Here's to the King—God bless him.

Here's to Liberty—may it never grow old.

Here's to friends—seen and unseen.

COLONIAL LEMONADE

Before the Revolution, John Hancock was one of the wealthiest men in Boston. His fortune rode the Atlantic winds: ships laden with sugar, molasses, rum, and citrus that linked the Caribbean, the Mediterranean, and the colonial wharves of New England. Among these treasures were lemons—rare, fragrant, and prized for their sharp flavor and their power to ward off scurvy on long voyages.

On Hancock's table, a glass of lemonade was more than a summer refreshment. It was a symbol of refinement, a visible sign of wealth drawn from the far corners of the empire. Yet by the 1760s and 1770s, those same lemons carried a different taste. British taxes on sugar and molasses—essential for lemonade and punch alike—struck directly at merchants such as Hancock. When he defied customs officials who tried to seize his cargo, he was defending more than his fortune. He was protecting a colonial way of life that found liberty not only in words, but in the freedom to trade, to taste, to live as one pleased.

A guest in Hancock's parlor might lift a glass of lemonade or lemon punch, tasting both the sweetness of hospitality and the bitterness of imperial control. In Revolutionary Boston, even a sip of lemonade could carry the flavor of defiance.

Original Receipt

Take the juice of two dozen lemons, add thereto two pounds of loaf sugar, and a quart of best white wine or rum, let it stand until the sugar be dissolved, then put to it three quarts of water, bottle it, and it will be fit for use.

Eighteenth-century lemonade was typically fortified with wine or spirits and was served to adults as a fashionable refreshment.

Modern Recipe

Skill Level: Easy
Prep Time: 10 minutes
Cook Time: 5 minutes
Total Time: 15 minutes (plus chilling)
Yield: Serves 4-6

COLONIAL LEMONADE (Continued)

Ingredients

- 1 cup fresh lemon juice (about 6 lemons)
- 1 cup sugar (or honey for variation)
- 1 cup white rum (optional, for adult punch version)
- 3 cups cold water or sparkling water
- Lemon slices and mint, for garnish

Directions

- In a small saucepan, combine the sugar and 1 cup of water.
- Heat gently, stirring, until the sugar dissolves completely.
- Remove from heat and let cool.
- In a pitcher, combine the lemon juice and cooled syrup.
- Add the remaining water (sparkling for variation) and stir well.
- For a punch, stir in the rum.
- Chill thoroughly.
- Serve chilled, garnished with lemon slices and mint.

Cook's Note: *In the 18th century, lemonade was rarely a children's drink. It was commonly fortified with wine or rum and served at social gatherings as a fashionable refreshment. Sugar and lemons were costly imports, making lemonade a quiet display of status as well as hospitality.*

REVOLUTIONARY RUM PUNCH

History is not always made in grand halls or on open battlefields. Sometimes it begins in the hush of an ordinary parlor.

On a winter afternoon in December 1773, as dusk crept over Boston, a small group of men gathered quietly to decide the fate of an empire. That evening would be remembered as the Boston Tea Party—but before the shouts and splashes in the harbor came the murmurs of conspiracy over a shared bowl of punch.

While the talk turned to ships, taxes, and defiance, in another room, a porcelain punchbowl was being filled and refilled. The sweet, potent mixture—rum, citrus, sugar, and resolve—was the silent companion to treason. It steadied hands and loosened tongues, a liquid oath shared among men who understood that what they planned could cost them everything.

Years later, **Peter Edes**, son of radical printer **Benjamin Edes**, recalled the scene to his grandson:

"I recollect perfectly well that in the afternoon preceding the evening of the destruction of the tea a number of gentlemen met in the parlor of my father's house… My station was in another room, to make punch for them in the bowl which is now in your possession, and which I filled several times."

In the eighteenth century, rum punch was more than a drink. It was the social language of the Atlantic world. Rum arrived in New England from Caribbean sugar plantations, tied to vast networks of trade and labor that bound the colonies to the British Empire even as they began to resist it. Punch—mixed communally and shared from a single bowl—was designed for conversation. It was meant to be lingered over, not hurried. Decisions were shaped in its presence.

The bowl itself mattered. So did the ladle, the careful balance of sweet and sharp, the slow refilling as the hours passed. In an age before formal meeting minutes or recorded votes, much of what guided the Revolution was spoken quietly and informally in rooms like this one. What was said over punch might never be written down—but it was remembered.

REVOLUTIONARY RUM PUNCH (Continued)

That December afternoon, the men who gathered knew the danger. To oppose Parliament was to invite arrest, ruin, or worse. Yet the setting remained domestic. A fire burned low. A bowl sat at the center of the room. Outside, the city carried on, unaware that plans were being laid which would soon echo across the harbor.

It is fitting that this moment survives not through official records but through the memory of a boy tasked with keeping the punch flowing. Peter Edes did not yet know he was witnessing history. He only knew to refill the bowl—again and again—for men who would soon slip into the night and change the course of the colonies.

Rum punch would continue to appear throughout the Revolution—at enlistments and celebrations, at councils and commemorations. It marked victories, softened losses, and bound people together in moments of uncertainty. Long after the tea sank beneath Boston Harbor, the memory of that shared bowl endured.

It reminds us that revolutions are not made by force alone. They are made in conversation, in conviction—and sometimes, in the quiet passing of a ladle from hand to hand.

Original Receipt

Take the Juice of fresh Lemons and put thereto fine Sugar, sufficient to sweeten it well. Add good West Indian rum, and a little Water to soften the strength. Grate in Nutmeg, if desired. Stir it well together in a Bowl, and taste it often, for Punch must be neither too sharp nor too weak, but of a proper Spirit.

Let it stand a little while before serving, that the flavors may marry. Serve in small glasses, or from the Bowl with a Ladle.

Modern Recipe

Skill Level: Easy
Prep Time: 20 minutes
Resting Time: 15 – 30 minutes (optional)
Total Time: 25 – 40 minutes
Yield: Serves 6 -8

REVOLUTIONARY RUM PUNCH (Continued)

Ingredients

- 1 cup fresh lemon juice (about 4–5 lemons)
- ¾ cup granulated sugar (or to taste)
- 2 cups dark rum
- 1½ cups cold water
- freshly grated nutmeg, for garnish

Directions

1. In a large bowl or pitcher, combine the lemon juice and sugar. Stir until the sugar is mostly dissolved.
2. Add the rum and cold water, stirring well.
3. Taste and adjust sweetness or strength as desired.
4. Chill briefly, or serve immediately over ice.
5. Let stand 15–30 minutes before serving, if time allows, to let the flavors marry. Finish with a light grating of nutmeg just before serving. Serve from a shared bowl or pitcher, with small glasses.

Cook's Note: *Eighteenth-century punch was mixed to taste rather than in fixed ratios. Hosts adjusted strength depending on the occasion—stronger for political company, lighter for long evenings of conversation.*

CLARET CUP
(COLONIAL SANGRIA)

In colonial America, punch was not merely a drink—it was a ceremony. No one understood the weight of that ritual better than Paul Revere, the Boston silversmith who made history with both silver and saddle. Among his most prized creations were gleaming silver punch bowls, raised in toasts by merchants, Masonic brothers, and Patriots alike.

Into those bowls went Claret Cup: French red wine brightened with sugar, citrus, and spice, sometimes fortified with brandy or fizzed with sparkling water. Light yet spirited, it carried the fragrance of refinement and the conviviality of shared purpose. To lift a ladle of claret cup from one of Revere's bowls was to taste both elegance and defiance—the sweetness of fellowship, the tartness of liberty.

In Boston's Green Dragon Tavern, where the Sons of Liberty plotted resistance, such bowls stood at the center of tables where conversation turned to conspiracy. Revere engraved freedom not only on paper and metal, but in ritual itself—giving his countrymen a vessel from which to drink unity before they forged it in revolution.

Today, Claret Cup feels familiar as a colonial sangria—red wine steeped with fruit and spice, served cold from a generous bowl. But in Revere's hands, it was more than refreshment. It was the taste of a nation in the making.

Figure 5. *Paul Revere, Sons of Liberty Bowl, 1768. Silver. Museum of Fine Arts, Boston (Accession no. 38.34).*

CLARET CUP (COLONIAL SANGRIA) (Continued)

Original Receipt

Take two bottles of Claret, and put it into a bowl, with the juice of two Seville oranges and a lemon, a quarter of a pound of fine sugar, a nutmeg grated, and a sprig of balm; let it stand about an hour, then strain it off, and put to it a quart of spring-water, and a glass of brandy.

Modern Recipe

Skill Level: Easy
Prep Time: 15 minutes
Chill (Standing)Time: 1 – 8 hours
Total Time: 1 hour 15 minutes to 8 hours 15 minutes
Yield: Serves 6

Ingredients

- 1 bottle (750 ml) dry red wine (claret-style Bordeaux, merlot, or cabernet franc works best)
- 1 orange, thinly sliced
- 1 lemon, thinly sliced
- 3 Tbsp sugar (or honey, to taste)
- ¼ tsp freshly grated nutmeg
- 1–2 oz brandy
- 1–2 sprigs fresh lemon balm or mint
- 1½–2 cups chilled sparkling water
- ice, for serving

  seasonal fruit (berries, apple slices) for garnish

Directions

1. In a large pitcher or bowl, combine wine, citrus slices, sugar, nutmeg, brandy, and herbs.
2. Stir gently until the sugar dissolves.
3. Refrigerate for at least 1 hour (up to 8 hours) to allow flavors to marry.

4. Just before serving, remove herbs and add sparkling water to taste.

5. Serve over ice in glasses, making sure each gets a slice of citrus.

Cook's Note: *Longer resting produces a softer, more integrated flavor. For brighter citrus notes, serve after 1–2 hours; for a deeper, rounder cup, allow it to stand overnight.*

WINE TODDY (MULLED WINE/NEGUS)

While Patriots toasted liberty with cider and ale, officers and Loyalists preferred something stronger: Negus, a warm wine toddy of claret, sugar, nutmeg, and lemon. Served in gleaming bowls at dinners and officers' messes, it was a drink of elegance and ceremony, more English than American. In occupied Philadelphia, no one poured it more freely than Benedict Arnold. As Military Governor in the winter of 1778, he filled his tables with wine and company, the scent of Negus rising with laughter and rumor alike. His entertainments dazzled the city but drained his purse, and his lavish wine bills became the talk of both friend and foe.

Negus, sweet and spiced, embodied Arnold himself—refined, ambitious, and fatally divided. What began as a gentleman's comfort became the emblem of his undoing: a cup raised too often, too proudly, over the slow ruin of loyalty.

Benedict Arnold, c. 1776. Portrait engraving after John Trumbull, Public Domain.

WINE TODDY (MULLED WINE/NEGUS) (Continued)

Original Mulled Wine/Negus Receipt

Boil a pint of water with a quarter of a pound of sugar and half a nutmeg grated; then add a pint of port and the juice of a lemon; stir it well together and serve it up hot.

Modern Recipe

Skill Level: Easy
Prep Time: 5 minutes
Cook Time: 10 minutes
Total Time: 15 minutes
Yield: Serves 2-3

Ingredients

- 2 cups of port wine

- 1 cup of water

- 3–4 Tbsp sugar, to taste

- Pinch of freshly grated nutmeg

- Strip of lemon peel (plus a little juice, if desired)

Variation – Negus (Wine Toddy):

- Add an equal part of water to the wine.

- Sweeten generously with sugar.

Directions

1. Combine the port wine and water in a small saucepan.

2. Warm gently over low heat until steaming, but do not boil.

3. Stir in the sugar until dissolved.

4. Add the lemon peel and a pinch of nutmeg.

5. Taste and adjust sweetness or citrus as needed.

6. Serve warm, with a light grating of nutmeg on top.

WINE TODDY (MULLED WINE/NEGUS) (Continued)

Historical Note

Negus was named for Colonel Francis Negus, a British officer, and became a fashionable drink among the elite. Lighter and more refined than punch, it was favored at banquets and winter gatherings in Britain and America.

Cook's Note: *Negus should be warmed slowly and never boiled. Boiling dulls the wine and drives off aroma—an error eighteenth-century writers warned against it repeatedly. The drink was meant to steam gently, not simmer, and to be consumed fresh rather than reheated. If you want a slightly more authentic profile, use a dry ruby port or light claret and err on the side of restraint with sugar; Negus was balanced, not syrupy.*

FLIP (HOT EGG AND SPIRIT DRINK)

In the smoky warmth of colonial taverns, where news, rumor, and revolution simmered beside pots of stew, one drink offered spectacle as much as solace: the Flip.

Born in the early eighteenth century and beloved by both farmers and Founding Fathers, Flip was a frothy concoction of ale, rum (or brandy), egg, sugar, and nutmeg—heated not by flame, but by plunging a red-hot iron into the mug. The result was theatrical: a hiss, a flare, and a rising froth that curled like breath over the hearth.

Washington drank Flip. So did sailors, innkeepers, and revolutionaries. It was served to ward off winter, to steady the nerves, to toast a victory—or to drown a defeat. Each fiery preparation drew silence, then applause. In that moment, a simple drink became a communal act of warmth and wonder.

Flip is the ancestor of eggnog and hot buttered rum, but unlike its creamy descendants, it carries fire in its blood and smoke in its breath.

Historical Note:

Taverns often kept iron rods by the hearth just for making Flip. Some inns even had dedicated "flip dogs"—iron implements shaped like pokers—passed from barkeep to barkeep like prized heirlooms.

FLIP (HOT EGG AND SPIRIT DRINK) (Continued)

Original Receipt

To make a Flip: take good ale and warm it near the fire. Beat an egg with sugar and mix in a dram of rum. Pour the liquor back and forth to froth or plunge a hot poker into the mixture until it hisses and foams. Drink hot.

Modern Recipe

Skill Level: Easy
Prep Time: 5 minutes
Cook Time: 5 - 10 minutes
Total Time: 10 – 15 minutes
Yield: Serves 1

Ingredients

- 12 oz ale or dark beer (porter or brown ale preferred)
- 1½ oz dark rum or brandy
- 1 whole egg
- 2 tsp brown sugar
- Freshly grated nutmeg, to taste

Directions

1. In a bowl, beat the egg with sugar and nutmeg until light and frothy.

2. Warm the ale in a saucepan until hot but not boiling. Remove from heat.

3. Slowly whisk the hot ale into the egg mixture to temper it and prevent curdling.

4. Stir in rum or brandy.

5. Pour into a heatproof mug.

6. (Optional, for authenticity) Plunge a red-hot iron rod into the drink (using tongs or a fire-safe handle) until it hisses and foams.

7. Serve immediately, while steaming.

FLIP (HOT EGG AND SPIRIT DRINK) (Continued)

Cook's Notes -*Flip variations included cream, molasses, or wine, depending on the tavern's region. Flip was sometimes served communally from a shared pewter tankard in early American inns.*

FLIP NON-ALCOHOLIC (COLONIAL-INSPIRED)

Original Receipt

Take Small Beer, or Water made hot, and beat an Egg very well with Sugar and a little grated Nutmeg. Pour the hot liquid gently into the Egg, stirring continually to prevent curdling. When well mixed, pour it back and forth between the vessels until it is thick and frothy. Drink it hot.

In the 18th century, Egg-based hot drinks were standard. They were served to children and the sick: pregnant women and the elderly.

Modern Recipe

Skill Level: Easy
Prep Time: 5 minutes
Cook Time: 5 minutes
Total Time: 10 minutes
Yield: Serves 1

Ingredients

- 12 oz dark malt beverage or strong brewed black tea

  barley malt drink (such as a malted milk–style beverage) or robust black tea.

- 1 whole egg
- 2 tsp brown sugar or molasses
- freshly grated nutmeg, to taste
- Optional: 1–2 Tbsp apple cider (for warmth and depth)

Directions

1. In a bowl, beat the egg with sugar and nutmeg until light and frothy.
2. Warm the malt beverage or tea until hot but not boiling.
3. Remove from heat.
4. Slowly whisk the hot liquid into the egg mixture to temper it and prevent curdling.
5. Stir well and pour into a heatproof mug.

FLIP NON-ALCOHOLIC (COLONIAL - INSPIRED (Continued)

6. (Optional, for authenticity) Froth vigorously by pouring back and forth between mugs.

7. Serve immediately while steaming. Cook's Note: For a closer eighteenth-century flavor, use a dark malt beverage rather than tea.

Cook's Note: *For a closer eighteenth-century flavor, use a dark malt beverage rather than tea.*

GLÜHWEIN
(TRADITIONAL GERMAN)

Hudson Valley, Winter 1778.

The wind howled like a widow through the bare trees of the Hudson Valley. In a drafty stone cellar beneath an occupied manor house, flickering lanterns cast long shadows over a makeshift gathering. Hessian mercenaries—German soldiers hired by the British—huddled together, homesick and bitter from the cold.

Among them was a cobbler's son from Hesse-Kassel named Dietrich Weiss, who had smuggled across the sea a small treasure: a scrap of paper, stained and creased, bearing his mother's recipe for *Glühwein—* mulled wine—the taste of home in winter.

Wine was scarce in the colonies, but the officers had stores of Burgundy, likely taken from Loyalist cellars. Oranges and lemons were rarities yet preserved peel arrived by barrel from the Caribbean. Spices—clove, cinnamon, nutmeg—were precious, hoarded for trade or stolen from captured ships. Brandy, at least, was plentiful, distilled by Dutch families who had never quite let go of their Old-World craft.

Dietrich heated the wine slowly, careful not to let it boil. He poured it into tin mugs, garnishing each with a curl of dried orange peel and a stick of cinnamon. The cellar filled with the scent of Christmas—of old worlds and lost homes. Even the officers softened.

One Hessian wrote home: "We drank a warm potion of wine and fire, brewed by Dietrich. For a moment, the war faded. I saw my brother's face again and heard bells from the market square."

Original Receipt

Take red wine and set it upon the fire till it is well heated but not boiled. Add thereto sugar, cinnamon, cloves, and a little ginger, with a strip of orange or lemon peel if it be had. Let it stand to draw and serve it hot.

GLÜHWEIN (TRADITIONAL GERMAN) (Continued)

<u>Modern Recipe</u>

Skill Level: Easy
Prep Time: 10 minutes
Cook Time: 45 minutes
Total Time: 55 minutes
Yield: Serves 4-5 quarts

Ingredients

- 2 bottles of dry red wine (Burgundy-style, Bordeaux, or Merlot)
- 1 orange, thinly sliced
- 1 lemon, thinly sliced
- ½ cup sugar, or to taste
- 3 cinnamon sticks
- 4–6 whole cloves
- ¼ tsp freshly grated nutmeg
- 1½ cups water
- ¼–½ cup brandy or dark rum (optional, added at the end)
- (Optional, modern accent: 1 star anise — use sparingly)

Directions

- Combine wine, water, sugar, citrus slices, and spices in a large pot.
- Heat gently over low heat, stirring until the sugar dissolves. Do not boil.
- Cover and let steep for 30–45 minutes, keeping the heat very low and never allowing it to simmer.
- Remove from heat. Stir in brandy or rum, if using.
- Strain and ladle into heatproof mugs. Garnish with citrus peel or a cinnamon stick.

HOLIDAYS & CELEBRATIONS

HOLIDAYS AND CELEBRATIONS

Holidays in Revolutionary America carried more than cheer; they carried meaning. In the eighteenth century, the colonial calendar was shaped by religious observances and civic festivals that, in wartime, took on new political life. What had once been familiar markers of the year became occasions freighted with uncertainty, hope, and resolve.

Christmas and New Years were the great winter holidays. Families and neighbors gathered for worship, feasts, and visits, even as war pressed in around them. In New England, Puritan suspicion of Old-World revelry had once muted Christmas, but by the time of the Revolution, cider, cakes, and puddings returned warmth to the season. New Year's Day brought social calls, small gifts, and the baking of seed cakes—rich with spice and caraway—offered as symbols of prosperity in the year ahead.

Thanksgiving, too, was transformed. Long observed as a day of prayer following harvests or deliverance, it became a patriotic act of gratitude. In 1777, after the American victory at Saratoga, the Continental Congress proclaimed a National Day of Thanksgiving—one of the first moments when people across the colonies were invited to pause and give thanks as a united cause. The table became a place not only for nourishment but also for national reflection.

After 1776, Independence Day became part of the calendar of festivals. It was marked by parades, cannon fire, bonfires, fireworks, and public readings of the Declaration of Independence. Even before peace was secured, the day served both as a commemoration and a promise—a reminder of what had been declared and what still remained to be won.

For soldiers, holidays were often observed far from home. In winter encampments and makeshift quarters, celebrations were improvised with what little could be spared: an extra ration saved, a shared bowl passed from tent to tent, a brief moment of warmth against the cold. Commanders understood that morale, like liberty itself, required tending. A holiday meal, however modest, restored spirits and reminded men of the lives waiting beyond the war.

For women, children, and the elderly, the keeping of holidays became an act of quiet resistance. To bake, to brew, to set a table despite shortages was to insist on continuity in a time of rupture. These rituals stitched together past and future, anchoring families to familiar rhythms even as the old order fell away. In kitchens and parlors across the colonies, Americans practiced independence long before it was secured season by season, dish by dish, holiday by holiday.

At every table, food and drink carried meaning. A bowl of punch spoke of fellowship. A seed cake offered hope for the future. A shared pudding or stew embodied endurance. In these ways, the holidays of the Revolution were never merely festive. They were declarations of identity, resilience, and the liberty Americans had only begun to taste.

GOVERNOR THOMAS HUTCHINSON'S PLUM PUDDING

Snow fell softly over the Massachusetts countryside as the grand houses of the colony prepared for Christmas in the English way: fires blazing, tables crowded with meats and pies, and—at the center of the feast—a steaming plum pudding.

No man in Boston embodied England's presence more than Governor Thomas Hutchinson, the royal governor. Once master of a mansion in the North End, he had watched it ransacked during the Stamp Act riots of 1765. Patriots smashed his furniture, tore down his curtains, and carried off his silver and heirlooms. Since then, Hutchinson had withdrawn to his country estate in Milton, governing from a safer distance, surrounded by loyal company and English comforts.

That same December, as patriots boarded ships at Griffin's Wharf and tossed more than three hundred chests of tea into Boston Harbor, Hutchinson's household celebrated Christmas in full Old-World fashion. At his table, plum pudding was more than a dessert—it was a declaration. Made with flour, suet, eggs, sugar, raisins, currants, nutmeg, and brandy, it drew upon the far-flung trade of Britain's empire: sugar from the West Indies, dried fruit from Europe, spirits from the mother country itself. Each bite was a taste of continuity, order, and allegiance.

For Hutchinson, plum pudding meant England—warm, sweet, and familiar on a cold Massachusetts night. For Boston's patriots, it was everything they opposed: taxes, monopolies, and imperial reach. As Hutchinson lifted a spoonful to his lips, rebellion was already stirring on the wharf—a different kind of heat rising from the harbor.

Original Receipt

Take a pound of flour, a pound of suet, shredded fine, a pound of raisins stoned, a pound of currants well washed and picked, half a pound of sugar, six eggs well beaten, a little salt, and a pint of milk. Mix all together, tie it in a floured cloth, and boil it for five hours.

— Elizabeth Raffald,
The Experienced English Housekeeper *(1769)*

GOVERNOR THOMAS HUTCHISON'S PLUM PUDDING (Continued)

<u>Modern Recipe</u>

Skill Level: Moderate
Prep Time: 30 minutes
Cook Time:1 hour 30 minutes
Total Time: 2 hours (plus resting)
Yield: Serves 6 -8

Ingredients

- 2 cups dried fruit (raisins, currants, cranberries, or chopped dates)
- zest of 1 orange or lemon
- ¼ cup brandy, rum, or apple cider (optional but recommended)
- 1 cup fresh breadcrumbs
- ½ cup brown sugar
- ½ cup melted butter
- 3 eggs, beaten
- ¾ cup milk
- 1 tsp cinnamon
- ½ tsp nutmeg
- ¼ tsp allspice or cloves
- ½ tsp salt

Directions

- Toss dried fruit with citrus zest and brandy (or cider).
- Let sit for 30 minutes.
- Preheat oven to 325°F (165°C). (A lower oven temperature ensures gentle, even cooking.)
- In a large bowl, mix breadcrumbs, sugar, spices, and salt.

GOVERNOR THOMAS HUTCHISON'S PLUM PUDDING
(Continued)

- Stir in butter, eggs, milk, and soaked fruit.

- Spoon into a greased loaf pan or pudding basin.

- Cover tightly with foil.

- Place the pan in a larger baking dish. Carefully pour hot water around it to reach about 1 inch up the sides (water bath)with 1 inch of hot water (water bath).

- Bake 90 minutes, until firm and darkened.

- Rest 10 minutes before slicing. Serve warm with custard or hard sauce; whipped cream is a later but acceptable addition.

Cook's Note - *Plum pudding in the eighteenth century was not a cake but a* **steamed or baked boiled pudding**—*dense, dark, and meant to keep. The water bath and long bake replicate the gentle heat of a hearth or boiling cloth. This pudding improves with rest and can be made a day ahead and reheated. Alcohol was common but not required; it served both as a flavoring and a preservative. The finished pudding should be firm, sliceable, and richly spiced, not light or fluffy.*

INDEPENDENCE CAKE

The summer of 1796 marked the 20th anniversary of the Declaration of Independence. Across the young United States, towns greeted the Fourth of July with cannon fire at dawn, bells at noon, and speeches in the public square. Families gathered afterward at long tables laden with roasted meats, pitchers of cider, and a new dessert that bore the very name of the cause they had fought for: Independence Cake.

The recipe appeared that same year in *American Cookery*, the first cookbook published in the United States. Its author, Amelia Simmons, was not a European chef but a domestic servant, writing for the kitchens of ordinary Americans. In giving her readers "Independence Cake," she offered more than a recipe—she offered a declaration of taste and nationhood.

Plum pudding, boiled in cloth as the English had done for centuries, symbolized the empire. Independence Cake, by contrast, was bold and spiced, baked high and fragrant. Sweetened with sugar or molasses, laced with brandy, wine, and cider, and heavy with raisins and currants, it was a cake made to be shared. Around it gathered a republic that prized the common table above the king's.

Each slice carried a message: Americans could feed themselves, celebrate themselves, and create their own traditions just as they had written their own laws. Liberty itself seemed baked into the flour and spice. What they tasted was not merely dessert, but the flavor of a nation—young, confident, and free.

<u>Original Receipt</u>

Independence Cake.—Three pounds of flour, one pound butter, one pound sugar, four eggs, one glass of wine, one glass of brandy, half pint emptins [yeast], one nutmeg, one tablespoon cinnamon, one-pound raisins, and one-pound currants. Make it as bread, put in fruit last, pour in half pint of cider; bake in large pans, two hours.

<u>Modern Recipe – Quick Bread Version</u>

Skill Level: Easy
Prep Time: 20 minutes
Cook Time: 75 – 90 minutes
Total Time: 2 hours (plus cooling)
Yield: Serves 1 large loaf or 2 standard loaves (12 – 14 servings)

INDEPENDENCE CAKE (Continued)

No yeast • No rising • Ready the same day

Ingredients

- 3½ cups all-purpose flour
- 1½ cups sugar (white or light brown)
- 1 cup unsalted butter, softened
- 4 large eggs, room temperature
- 1 cup apple cider (or half cider, half milk)
- ¼ cup brandy (optional but traditional)
- 2 tsp baking powder
- ½ tsp baking soda
- 1 tsp cinnamon
- ½ tsp nutmeg
- ½ tsp salt
- 1½ cups raisins
- 1½ cups currants (or dried cranberries)

Directions

- Preheat oven to 325°F (165°C). Grease a large loaf pan or two standard loaf pans. (Lower temperature ensures even baking for dense, fruit-rich cakes.)
- Cream butter and sugar until light and fluffy.
- Beat in eggs one at a time.
- Stir in cider and brandy.
- In a separate bowl, whisk flour, baking powder, baking soda, spices, and salt.
- Add dry ingredients to the wet mixture gradually. The batter will be thick.
- Fold in raisins and currants.
- Spoon into prepared pan(s). Smooth the top.

INDEPENDENCE CAKE (Continued)

- Bake 75–90 minutes (single large loaf) or 60–70 minutes (two loaves), until a tester comes out clean.

- Cool completely before slicing. Flavor improves overnight.

Inspired by an eighteenth-century Independence Cake.

Cook's Note: *Independence Cake is closer to a fruit-studded bread than a modern layer cake. It is dense, lightly sweet, and improves with rest. For the best flavor, bake a day ahead and store tightly wrapped. Traditionally served in slices with cider or wine rather than frosting.*

WASSAIL CHRISTMAS HOLIDAY PUNCH

In December 1775, Boston was under British occupation. General William Howe, commander of the British forces, presided over a town ringed by Patriot militia, its harbor blockaded, its people worn thin by war. Yet within the warmth of British quarters, officers clung to the rituals of England.

At Christmas, those rituals gathered around the wassail bowl. Into great silver or earthen vessels went hot ale and cider, spiced with nutmeg, ginger, and cinnamon, sweetened with sugar, and crowned with roasted apples. The steaming punch was ladled into cups raised in loyal toasts—not to Boston, nor to liberty, but to the King's health and victory for the empire.

For the soldiers who filled Howe's ranks, wassail was more than a drink. It was a taste of home: of English hearths far away, of candlelight and holly, of families gathered beyond the sea. Outside those walls, Patriots faced a brutal New England winter with little more than plain cider and hard bread. The wassail bowl stood as a symbol of the divide itself—the comforts of occupation within, the hunger of rebellion without.

Source: Victorian engraving, 19th century. Public domain.

<u>Original Receipt</u>

To make a Wassail, boil ale, put in sugar, nutmeg, and ginger; then take toast cut thin, soak them in the ale, put them into a bowl, with roasted crab-apples; pour the ale over them.

Modern Recipe

Skill Level: Easy
Prep Time: 10 minutes
Cook Time: 15-20 minutes
Total Time: 25-30 minutes
Yield: Serves About 10 – 12 cups

Ingredients

- 2 quarts of apple cider

- 2 cups of ale (or additional cider)

- ⅓–½ cup brown sugar, to taste

- 2 tsp ground ginger

- 1 tsp nutmeg

- 2 cinnamon sticks

- 4–6 small tart apples, roasted until skins split

- toasted bread slices (optional, traditional)

Directions

- Warm cider and ale with sugar and spices until steaming; do not boil.

- Place roasted apples and toast in a large heatproof bowl.

- Pour the hot cider mixture over them.

- Ladle into mugs and serve hot.

Cook's Note: *Wassail was traditionally served communally from a large bowl, often with roasted apples and toasted bread floating in the punch. The drink should be hot but never boiling, which preserves the flavor of the cider and ale. In colonial households, wassail was ladled slowly and lingered over rather than consumed quickly.*

Did you know?

- The real George Washington Delaware crossing was on Dec. 25–26, 1776 (started at 6:00 pm and finished at 4:00 am.)
- Took place during a severe nor'easter with blizzard conditions.
- Soldiers were ordered to stay low to balance the boats
- Washington would have been hunched and nost standing, cloaked, and bracing against the storm
- The iconic "heroic pose" was added in 1851 to inspire mid-19th-century audiences and emphasize symbolic leadership.

Source: Washington's Christmas Miracle Crossing Delaware Public Domain

ELECTION CAKE

Even before Independence Day, Election Day in colonial Hartford was no quiet affair. In 1771, it was equal parts politics, carnival, and chaos. Men in tricorn hats crowded the green, having ridden for miles to cast their votes—or simply to witness the spectacle. Alehouses brimmed, fiddlers played, and from every kitchen hearth drifted the rich scent of yeast, spice, and rising dough.

At the center of it all stood the famed Election Cake, baked in loaves so large they could feed entire militias. Women worked through the night, kneading vast quantities of dough, creaming butter and sugar by hand, and stirring in precious spices, brandy, and fruit. The cake was their offering to the body politic—a feast prepared not for themselves, but for the men who fancied themselves builders of a new nation.

But where there was cake, there was also scandal. One Hartford tavern keeper was rumored to have slipped more than brandy into her recipe. Soldiers swore her slices made them "frisk as colts," and neighbors whispered that her cake drew more men than the polling place itself. A pamphleteer later joked that *the people were more taken with the pudding of her house than with the principles of the state.*

By the time the Revolution arrived, Election Cake had become both sustenance and symbol—a patriotic loaf, a festive indulgence, and, on occasion, a scandalous delight. To eat a slice was to participate in civic life, to mark the ritual of self-government with spice and sweetness. It was democracy, quite literally, baked into the day—where politics, pleasure, and the promise of liberty rose together in the same oven.

<u>Original Receipt</u>

In a large bowl mix flour and a portion of sugar. Add warm milk and yeast, and work into a soft dough. When it has risen, light, work in softened butter, remaining sugar, beaten eggs, dried fruit (raisins or currants), and spices such as cinnamon, nutmeg, and allspice. Knead well and let rise again. Shape into loaves or large round cakes and let rest until light. Bake in a moderate oven until cooked through and richly browned.

Election Cake was baked in quantity to feed voters and celebrate Election Day and was often served at communal gatherings. It intentionally omits exact quantities to echo the feel of historical household receipts, which often worked by feel and crowd size.

ELECTION CAKE (Continued)

<u>Modern Recipe</u>

Skill Level: Moderate
Prep Time: 30 minutes
Rise Time: 1½ - 2 hours
Bake Time: 40 – 50 minutes
Total Time: About 2½ - 3 hours
Yield: Serves 1 load or round cake serves 8-10

Ingredients

- 3 cups of all-purpose flour
- 1 cup warm whole milk (about 110°F)
- 2¼ tsp active dry yeast (1 packet)
- ½ cup packed brown sugar
- ½ cup unsalted butter, softened
- 2 large eggs, room temperature
- 1 cup raisins or currants
- 1 tsp ground cinnamon
- ½ tsp ground nutmeg
- ¼ tsp ground allspice
- ½ tsp salt
- Optional: 2–4 tbsp brandy or sweet wine (for richness)

Directions

1. Warm the milk until just warm to the touch. Sprinkle in the yeast and a teaspoon of sugar; let stand 5–10 minutes until foamy.

2. In a large bowl, combine 2 cups of flour, brown sugar, and salt. Add the yeast mixture and stir to combine.

3. Add the softened butter and eggs; beat until smooth. Stir in raisins and spices.

4. Gradually mix in the remaining flour until you have a soft, slightly sticky dough.

ELECTION CAKE (Continued)

5. Cover and let rise in a warm place until doubled in size, about 1–1½ hours.

6. Punch down the dough, shape into a loaf or place in a greased cake pan and let rise 30–45 minutes more.

7. Bake at 350°F (175 °C) for 40–50 minutes, until golden and cooked through. Cool before slicing.

Serving Tip: Election Cake keeps well and improves in flavor over 1–2 days — just like its historic ancestors.

Cook's Note: *Election Cake is closer to a lightly sweetened, spiced bread than a modern dessert cake. It is sturdy, fragrant, and improves after a day's rest. Traditionally baked in large loaves or rounds to feed crowds, it was often served plain or with cider—never frosted.*

NEW YEAR'S SEED CAKE

As the calendar turned to a new year, colonial families marked the season with gatherings of neighbors, friends, and political allies. On their tables, one dish appeared again and again: the seed cake. Rich with butter, eggs, and sugar, and flavored with caraway seeds, the cake was festive, substantial, and deeply symbolic. In English tradition, seeds represented fertility, prosperity, and growth—a fitting emblem for New Year's and Twelfth Night celebrations.

In Boston, where politics and sociability were never far apart, Samuel Adams and John Hancock often welcomed fellow patriots at holiday open houses. Food and drink were as central to Revolutionary life as pamphlets and speeches. A well-made seed cake, set beside bowls of punch or spiced cider, offered not only refreshment but a reminder of continuity—an English custom adapted to the uncertain promise of America's future.

Though little known in America today, seed cakes are still baked in Britain and Ireland as heritage confections. Their symbolic use of seeds endures in modern New Year's traditions, where foods are eaten for good fortune in the year ahead. Whether flavored with the sharp bite of caraway or the gentler sweetness of poppy seeds, seed cake offers both a taste of the Revolution and a hopeful beginning to the year to come.

Original Receipt

Take a pound of butter, beat it with your hand till it is soft like cream, then beat in a pound of loaf sugar very fine, twelve eggs well beaten, and put in a pound of flour, two ounces of carraway-seeds, beat all well together, butter your pan, and put it in, and bake it an hour in a quick oven.

Modern Recipe

Skill Level: Easy - Moderate
Prep Time: 20 minutes
Cook Time: 45 – 44 minutes
Total Time: 1 hour 15 minutes
Yield: Serves 1 loaf (8 – 10 slices)

NEW YEAR'S SEED CAKE (Continued)

Ingredients

- 1 cup (2 sticks) unsalted butter, softened
- 1 ½ cups sugar
- 4 eggs
- 2 cups all-purpose flour
- 2 tsp baking powder
- ½ tsp salt
- 1 cup sour cream (or plain Greek yogurt)
- 2 tbsp caraway seeds *(traditional)* or poppy seeds *(modern variation)*
- 1 tsp vanilla extract
- Optional: zest of 1 lemon or orange

Directions

1. Preheat oven to 350°F (175°C). Grease and flour a loaf or bundt pan.
2. Cream butter and sugar together until light and fluffy.
3. Beat in eggs one at a time.
4. In a separate bowl, whisk together flour, baking powder, and salt. Add to wet mixture in thirds, alternating with the sour cream, beginning and ending with flour.
5. Stir in the seeds (caraway for the original flavor, or poppy seeds for a modern twist), vanilla, and citrus zest, if using.
6. Pour the mixture into the prepared pan and bake for 45–55 minutes, until golden brown and a toothpick inserted in the center comes out clean.
7. Cool before slicing.

NEW YEAR'S SEED CAKE (Continued)

Cook's Note - *Seed Cake is not overly sweet and is meant to be served plain, without frosting. Caraway was the traditional flavor in the eighteenth century, prized for both taste and digestion; poppy seeds offer a gentler, modern alternative. This cake improves after several hours of rest and was often served in thin slices with tea, cider, or wine to mark the turning of the year.*

COLONIAL HOSTING
& TABLE CUSTOMS

COLONIAL HOSTING & TABLE CUSTOMS

In the eighteenth century, the table was more than a place to eat. It was one of the few spaces where daily life, social order, labor, belief, and community converged. Meals carried meaning far beyond nourishment. They instructed children, affirmed hierarchy, bound neighbors, and reflected the rhythms of work and survival.

Colonial hosting was not extravagant by modern standards. It was restrained, deliberate, and shaped by necessity. Yet within that restraint existed a deep sense of responsibility. To host was to provide not only food, but order. To sit at a table was to participate in a shared understanding of place and behavior.

Food did not arrive at the table, already separated into courses or portions. Instead, dishes were placed at the center and shared. Bread, stews, puddings, meats, and vegetables were meant to be taken in moderation, with awareness of others—the act of eating reinforced the values of economy and consideration. One took no more than was proper, and waste was quietly discouraged.

This communal style of eating was born of practicality, but it carried social weight. Sharing food reinforced bonds within the household and among guests. It reminded each person at the table that survival was collective. Even in households of relative comfort, abundance was not taken for granted. The table reflected what the season, the land, and the circumstances allowed.

Seating, too, followed an unspoken logic. The head of the household often occupied the end of the table, not as a gesture of dominance, but of responsibility. Elders and honored guests were seated closest. Children frequently stood or sat apart, observing before participating fully. Placement conveyed respect, age, and standing within the family or community.

This hierarchy was rarely explained aloud. It was learned through repetition. Children absorbed it by watching. Guests understood it instinctively. The table quietly mirrored the structure of the broader colonial world, where order was believed necessary for stability.

Conversation during meals was measured. In many households, silence during the main course was customary. This was not a sign of discomfort or severity, but of attention. Food represented labor — hours of work at the hearth, in the field, or at the mill. Quiet eating acknowledged that labor. Conversation often followed only after the table was cleared, when the demands of the meal had passed.

Daily fare was plain and sustaining. Most meals consisted of porridge, bread, stews, and modest portions of meat or vegetables when available. These meals were functional, designed to fuel work rather than entertain. Eating was regular, purposeful, and brief.

Feasts stood apart from this daily rhythm. They were rare and, therefore, meaningful. Holidays, weddings, elections, religious observances, or the arrival of important guests justified extra effort. Additional dishes appeared. Sweets and puddings were served. Drink flowed more freely. The table expanded, both in size and spirit.

Abundance, when it appeared, carried symbolic weight. It marked gratitude, celebration, or honor. Its rarity gave it power. A feast was remembered not because it was lavish, but because it was exceptional.

Hospitality in the colonial world was not optional. Travelers were fed. Neighbors were welcomed. Even households with limited means were expected to offer what they could. Refusing hospitality was considered a social failure. To host was to uphold one's standing within the community.

This expectation shaped behavior as much as menus. Food was stretched. Dishes were shared. Guests were made comfortable even when resources were thin. Hospitality was not about display, but about inclusion.

As evening gatherings extended beyond the meal, the tone often softened. Candles were refreshed. Furniture might be moved aside. Music — a fiddle, flute, or simple singing — filled the room. Dancing sometimes followed, especially on celebratory occasions. These were not performances, but communal expressions. Participation mattered more than skill.

Even then, restraint remained. Movement was structured. Music supported the fellowship rather than dominating it. The evening unfolded gradually, guided by candlelight and conversation rather than clock or schedule.

Colonial hosting balanced formality with warmth. The rules that governed the table were not meant to intimidate, but to maintain harmony. Order created comfort. Predictability allowed generosity to flourish within constraints.

Understanding these customs reveals why colonial recipes are written the way they are. They assume sharing. They assume restraint. They assume a table shaped by season, scarcity, and community rather than choice alone.

Feasts stood apart from this daily rhythm. They were rare and, therefore, meaningful. Holidays, weddings, elections, religious observances, or the arrival of important guests justified extra effort. Additional dishes appeared. Sweets and puddings were served. Drink flowed more freely. The table expanded, both in size and spirit.

The active compound in willow bark, salicin, would later be identified and refined into acetylsalicylic acid (aspirin), one of the most widely used and studied medicines in the modern world.

To recreate colonial food without acknowledging how it was served is to miss its deeper meaning. The recipes fed bodies, but the table shaped lives. The customs of the table, like the food itself, were shaped by forces beyond preference — by season, labor, and survival. To understand what appeared on the table, one must next understand when it appeared at all.

A colonial table was set for sharing rather than individual service. Knives were essential, forks uncommon, and the center of the table mattered more than any single place.

Colonial tables did not follow the standardized place settings familiar today. There were no assigned forks, no symmetrical arrangements, and no expectation of individual portions.

Meals were organized *around* shared dishes placed at the center of the table. Knives were considered essential and were often carried by the diner. Forks were uncommon, and, when present, used primarily for serving. Spoons were shared, especially for stews and porridges.

This arrangement reflected both practicality and values. The table emphasized economy, restraint, and awareness of others. How one ate mattered as much as what one ate.

Illustrative reconstruction of an 18th-century table setting

SEASONS & SURVIVAL

SEASONS & SURVIVAL

Colonial cooking followed the land, not the calendar.

Food did not arrive at the table by choice or preference, but by season and circumstance. Ingredients appeared and disappeared according to weather, labor, and harvest. Recipes existed not to provide variety, but to answer necessity. Survival depended on knowing when to eat fresh, when to preserve, and when to endure scarcity.

The year unfolded slowly, and the table changed with it.

Spring, to modern eyes, suggests renewal and abundance. The weather softens. The earth awakens. Green returns to the fields. Yet for colonial households, spring was often the most uncertain and difficult time of the year.

Winter stores—carefully preserved through months of cold—were nearly exhausted. Root cellars emptied. Salted meat thinned. Grain bins ran low. What had been saved with care now had to last just a little longer. At the same time, the land had not yet begun to give back. Seeds were planted, not harvested. Gardens were bare or newly sprouted. Though the fields promised food, the table remained sparse.

Labor increased sharply in the spring. Fields were plowed. Fences repaired. Crops planted. Bodies worked harder precisely when nourishment was most limited. Foraged greens—nettles, dandelion, sorrel—offered freshness and relief, but not sustenance. Meals were stretched. Porridges thinned. Bread eaten sparingly. Waste was unthinkable.

Historians refer to this period as the spring hunger gap—a recurring pattern in regions where people depend directly on the land. Spring brought hope to the fields, but hunger to the table.

Relief arrived gradually as summer took hold.

Gardens began to yield. Milk returned. Butter, eggs, vegetables, and fruit reappeared. Meals grew lighter and faster, shaped by heat and the demands of fieldwork. Food was eaten soon after harvest, with little thought to preservation. Cooking emphasized immediacy rather than storage, nourishment rather than endurance.

Summer abundance was enjoyed but never trusted to last. Colonists understood that plenty was temporary. Even in times of relative comfort, the table reflected awareness rather than excess. Fresh foods appeared briefly, then vanished again. What could not be eaten quickly was already being considered for later seasons.

As summer faded, urgency replaced ease.

Autumn was the most consequential season of the year. It determined survival. Crops were gathered. Livestock slaughtered. Fruit dried. Vegetables stored. Meat salted, smoked, or rendered into fat. Preservation was not a craft or a preference—it was a necessity.

Families worked to ensure nothing spoiled or was wasted. The winter table depended entirely on autumn's success. Salting, smoking, drying, fermenting, and cool storage transformed fresh food into sustenance. These methods allowed it to endure months of cold and darkness.

Autumn cooking was shaped less by pleasure than by responsibility. Each task carried a consequence. Each failure echoed forward into winter.

When winter arrived, the table narrowed.

Fresh food disappeared almost entirely. Meals relied on what endured: salted meat, dried fruit, grains, beans, and root vegetables. Cooking emphasized warmth and fullness—stews, puddings, baked dishes, and breads meant to nourish and fortify.

Variety was limited. Substitution was expected. Ingenuity mattered more than abundance. The hearth became the center of the household, and the table reflected patience and resilience rather than choice.

Yet even in winter, the table did not disappear. Meals continued. Families gathered. Food, though simple, sustained not only bodies but routine and connection.

Across the year, colonial cooks did not ask what they wanted to eat. They asked what the season allowed.

Recipes were shaped by weather, labor, and survival rather than preference. Substitution was not a failure. Preservation was not optional. Restraint was not deprivation, but wisdom.

To cook historically is to recognize that abundance is fragile, and that knowledge—not excess—sustains a table.

Even in a modern kitchen where ingredients seem endlessly available, the lessons of seasonality remain. To cook seasonally is to cook with awareness. And awareness, in any century, is the beginning of good food.

POTTAGE WITH EARLY GREENS

Spring: The Hunger Gap

This simple pottage reflects what many colonial households relied upon in early spring, when winter stores were thinning, and gardens had not yet begun to yield. Barley was valued for its ability to stretch, to fill, and to nourish when little else was available. Early foraged greens—nettles, sorrel, dandelion, or young spinach—brought freshness after months of preserved food, though they added more relief than sustenance. This dish is not meant to impress. It is meant to endure.

Original Receipt:

Take barley well cleaned, boil it in fair water till it is tender; add such herbs as are first to spring, with enough salt, and serve hot.

Modern Recipe:

Skill Level: Easy
Prep Time: 10 minutes
Cook Time: 50 minutes
Total Time: 1 hour
Yield: Serves 4

Ingredients:

- ½ cup pearl barley

- 4 cups water or light broth

- 1 cup early greens (spinach, sorrel, dandelion greens, or chard), chopped

- ½ teaspoon salt (or to taste)

- Optional: a small knob of butter or a drizzle of oil for serving

Directions:

1. Rinse the barley thoroughly under cold water.
2. Place the barley and water (or broth) in a pot and bring it to a gentle boil.

POTTAGE WITH EARLY GREENS (Continued)

3. Reduce the heat and simmer, uncovered, for 40–45 minutes, until the barley is tender and the liquid thickens to a light porridge.
4. Stir in the salt.
5. Add the greens and cook for an additional 5–7 minutes, just until they wilt and soften.
6. Serve hot, plain, or finish with a small amount of butter or oil if desired.

***Cook's Notes** - A splash of vinegar at the table reflects a common colonial practice and brightens the dish. Mixing wild and cultivated greens mirrors historical scarcity and the seasonal transition of early spring. Leftovers thicken as they cool and are often reheated the following day with a little added water.*

Scarcity & Substitution

When barley was unavailable, oats or rye were used in much the same way. Greens varied widely by region and season; whatever appeared first in the field or garden was welcomed.

Spring brought renewed labor before renewed abundance. Pottages like this allowed households to stretch what remained, conserve resources, and endure until summer returned fresh food to the table.

Summer: Abundance & Immediacy

Summer arrived not with ceremony, but with relief.

After the uncertainty of spring, the land finally gave back. Gardens filled. Fields greened. Milk returned to the table. Eggs, vegetables, and fruit appeared again after months of restraint. The hunger gap eased, not all at once, but steadily, as each new harvest replaced what had long been absent.

Summer food was shaped by immediacy. What the land offered was eaten quickly, often within hours of gathering. Little effort was spent on preservation during these months. There would be time for that later. For now, the priority was nourishment and speed.

The heat discouraged long cooking. Ovens were avoided when possible. Meals were simpler, lighter, and faster to prepare, shaped by the demands of fieldwork and the limits of the season. Food needed to sustain labor without exhausting fuel or time.

Cabbage, one of the most dependable crops, appeared frequently at the summer table. Hardy, abundant, and easily stored for short periods, it could be eaten fresh or lightly dressed. Vinegar and salt brought brightness and balance after months of preserved fare. Herbs from the garden added freshness without excess.

Summer abundance was enjoyed—but never assumed permanent.

Colonial households understood that plenty was temporary. Each fresh dish carried an awareness of what had come before and what would follow. Even in moments of relief, restraint remained.

Food in summer was not meant to impress. It was meant to restore.

Meals during these months offered contrast: cool against heat, fresh against preserved, simple against sustaining. The body recovered. The household breathed. The table widened briefly before narrowing again. Summer cooking reminds us that abundance does not need embellishment. When food is fresh and timely, little else is required. The dishes of this season speak quietly of balance — between labor and nourishment, between gratitude and foresight. They exist not to mark celebration, but to meet the moment fully, before it passes.

CABBAGE SLAW WITH VINEGAR & HERBS

Original Receipt:

Slice the cabbage very small, add vinegar and salt, with herbs as you like; let it stand a little, and serve fresh.

Modern Recipe:

Skill Level: Easy
Prep Time: 10 minutes
Cook Time: 0 minutes
Resting Time: 10 - 15 minutes
Total Time: 20-25 minutes
Yield: Serves 4

Ingredients:

- 4 cups green or white cabbage, finely sliced
- 2 tablespoons apple cider vinegar
- ½ teaspoon salt, or to taste
- 1 tablespoon fresh herbs, finely chopped (parsley, chives, dill, or a combination)
- Optional: 1 tablespoon oil or melted butter

Directions:

1. Place the sliced cabbage in a bowl and sprinkle with salt.
2. Add the vinegar and toss gently to combine.
3. Stir in the herbs and, if using, the oil or butter.
4. Allow the slaw to stand for 10–15 minutes before serving, just until softened.
5. Serve cool or at room temperature.

CABBAGE SLAW WITH VINEGAR & HERBS (Continued)

Cook's Notes *- This slaw was often served alongside hot dishes to balance heavier fare. Allowing the cabbage to stand softens it without cooking, a common practice in warm months.*

Autumn: The Urgency of the Harvest

Autumn was not a single moment, but a narrowing window.

Between the ease of summer and the endurance of winter lay a brief, demanding season when abundance arrived all at once—and threatened to vanish just as quickly. Fields, gardens, and orchards delivered their final gifts in close succession, each requiring immediate attention. What could not be eaten, dried, baked, or preserved would be lost.

Among the most fleeting of these gifts were cherries.

Cherries ripen quickly and spoil faster than most fruits. Their season was short, their sweetness fragile, and their abundance overwhelming when it arrived. Unlike apples or squash, cherries offered little forgiveness. To delay was to waste. To hesitate was to lose them entirely.

For this reason, cherries were not treated as luxuries. They were treated as problems to be solved.

Households responded quickly rather than with refinement. Cherries were pitted, baked, or cooked almost immediately, transformed into dishes meant to arrest their decline, if only briefly. Baking did not preserve cherries for the winter in the way drying or salting preserved other foods, but it extended their usefulness and prevented immediate loss.

This urgency defined autumn cooking. It was a season of judgment and action. Fruit was not chosen for elegance, but for necessity. Sugar was used sparingly. Pastry was rustic. The goal was not celebration, but stewardship.

AUTUMN THE URGENCY OF THE HARVEST (Continued)

Cherry dishes of the season reflected this mindset. They were simple, quickly assembled, and meant to be eaten soon. They stood at the

threshold between summer abundance and autumn responsibility, marking the moment when the household turned from enjoyment to preparation.

The table in autumn carried weight. Each dish represented labor already spent and labor yet to come. Cherries, bright and fleeting, reminded cooks that not all abundance could be saved — only managed.

In this way, cherries belong to autumn not as a symbol of plenty, but as a lesson in restraint and urgency. It appears briefly, demands action, and disappears again, leaving behind the preservation work that would sustain the household through the months ahead. The dish that follows reflects this moment of decision — cherries at their peak, quickly transformed, not for indulgence but to prevent their loss.

CHERRY PANDOWDY

Original Receipt:

Lay the cherries in a deep dish, sweeten to taste, and add a little flour to thicken the juice. Cover with a plain paste and bake in a moderate oven. When the crust has set, break it into pieces and return it to the oven until the juices are thick and well mixed. Serve warm.

Modern Recipe:

Skill Level: Moderate
Prep Time: 20 minutes
Cook Time: 40 – 45 minutes
Total Time: 1 hour
Yield: Serves 6

Ingredients:

- 4 cups fresh or frozen cherries, pitted
- ½–¾ cup sugar (to taste)
- 2 tbsp butter, cut into pieces
- 1½–2 tbsp all-purpose flour or cornstarch
- 1 tbsp apple cider (preferred) or water
- ½ tsp cinnamon or nutmeg (optional)
- 1 thick pie crust or biscuit-style dough

Directions:

1. Preheat oven to 375°F.
2. Place cherries in a deep baking dish or cast-iron skillet.
3. Toss with sugar, spices (if using), butter, and cider.
4. Lay crust loosely over the fruit; do not crimp or seal.
5. Bake for 20–25 minutes, until juices bubble.
6. Remove from the oven and break the crust into the fruit with a spoon.

7. Return to oven and bake another 20–25 minutes, until browned and thickened.
8. Serve hot, with cream or vanilla custard if desired.

Cook's Notes - *Pandowdy was intentionally rustic; breaking the crust allowed fruit juices to thicken naturally. This dish was meant to be eaten soon after baking, not stored.*

WINTER: ENDURANCE & INGENUITY

Winter was the great test of survival in the eighteenth century. Once the fields lay bare and rivers froze, the work of the year was finished—and its success, or failure, revealed itself at the table. For colonial families, winter eating was shaped not by choice but by preparation. What endured the cold was what endured the season.

Pantries filled with barrels of salted beef and pork, dried peas and beans, grains stored in sacks, apples packed in straw, and root vegetables buried deep in cellars. Smokehouses perfumed the air with the scent of hams and fish cured to prevent spoilage. Milk vanished with the frost, replaced by hard cheeses and butter preserved with salt. Fresh greens were rare; their absence was keenly felt after months of relying on meat and starch.

Yet winter food was not without comfort. Long nights drew families inward, and meals grew heavier, warmer, and more sustaining. Stews simmered for hours, puddings boiled patiently by the hearth, and bread rose slowly in kitchens warmed by fire rather than sun. Spices—nutmeg, ginger, cinnamon—appeared more often now, adding warmth and fragrance to otherwise plain fare.

Holiday tables offered moments of indulgence amid restraint. Christmas, New Year's, and Twelfth Night were marked by special dishes drawn from English tradition: plum puddings, seed cakes, wassail bowls, and celebratory breads. These foods were not every day fare, but deliberate pauses—ritual reminders of continuity, community, and hope during the year's darkest days.

Winter taught endurance. It rewarded foresight and punished waste. To eat well in winter was not to eat abundantly, but wisely—to stretch stores, share generously, and trust that the cycle would turn again. When spring finally returned, it was not merely a season, but a triumph.

In the cold months following autumn slaughter, pork appeared often

at winter tables, roasted slowly and paired with apples drawn from cellar stores. The combination of savory meat and sweet fruit was a hallmark of early American cooking, offering both nourishment and comfort during the year's darkest season.

JUICY GARLIC HERB PORK LOIN

Original Receipt:

To Roast Pork.

Take a loin, leg, or chine of pork, score the skin, and rub it well with salt. Roast it before a clear fire, basting often. When nearly done, dredge it in flour and baste again to make a crisp, crackling crust. Serve it with apples sliced and stewed, or roasted in the dripping-pan, and send it to the table very hot.

Modern Recipe:

Skill Level: Easy
Prep Time: 10 – 15 minutes
Cook Time: 55 – 65 minutes
Total Time: About 1 hour 15 minutes
Yield: Serves: 4 - 6

Ingredients:

- 1½–2 pounds pork loin (Best Cut is pork loin, not tenderloin)
- 2 tbsp olive oil
- 2 tbsp butter, cut into pieces
- 4 cloves garlic, smashed
- 1 tsp kosher salt
- 1 tsp black pepper
- 1 tsp dried thyme or rosemary (or a mix)
- 1 cup chicken broth (or pork broth)
- Optional: ½ cup white wine or apple cider
- Optional: ½ onion, sliced (for extra au jus)

Directions:

1. Preheat oven to 325°F.
2. Season pork generously on all sides with salt, pepper, and herbs.
3. Sear pork

JUICY GARLIC HERB PORK LOIN

4. Heat olive oil in an oven-safe skillet or Dutch oven over medium-high heat.

5. Sear pork on all sides until golden brown, about 2–3 minutes per side.

6. Add liquid

7. Reduce the heat to medium.

8. Add garlic, butter, broth, and wine or cider if using.

9. Spoon liquid over pork.

10. Cover tightly with lid or foil.

11. Transfer to the oven and roast for 45–60 minutes, until the internal temperature reaches 140–145°F.

Cook's Note *–Pork benefits from a short rest after roasting. Let it stand, lightly covered, before slicing, that the juices may return to the meat.*

CLOSING REFLECTIONS

In the kitchens of the Revolution, history was not written with ink alone. It was stirred into pots, kneaded into loaves, and ladled into bowls around hearths that never cooled.

Families gathered, soldiers rested, and strangers became neighbors over food that was simple, sustaining, and sacred to survival. These recipes tell the story of an America in the making—of women who stretched rations into miracles, of allies who brought new flavors and old traditions, and of communities who gave what they had so that liberty might endure.

In every loaf of bread, in each spoonful of stew, lies a reminder: history is not merely something we inherit, but something we keep alive. As our nation marks milestones of remembrance—from the 250th anniversary and beyond—these stories and recipes remind us that anniversaries may pass, but their meaning endures. What remains are the tables we gather at, the food we share, and the memory of those who came before.

The Revolution was fought with muskets and words, but it endured with food and fellowship. And so, it remains today.

This cookbook was written to honor those often-forgotten voices whose hands performed the quiet labor of a revolution. Their kitchens were as vital as the battlefields, their tables as crucial as the halls of government. In recovering their dishes, we recover their stories—and recognize that freedom was not won by generals alone, but by bakers, farmers, cooks, and servants who fed the dream of independence.

May cooking these meals today make you feel part of that unbroken chain—a table stretching from the eighteenth century to our own. To set a dish before family or friends is to keep faith with those who once did the same in far leaner times.

For readers who wish to deepen their experience of Revolutionary era cooking, a curated playlist of period-inspired music is available below. Simply scan the QR code to let the echoing the sounds of Revolutionary kitchens, camps, and taverns fill your cooking space. Let it play as you cook, gather, and reflect on the endurance, fellowship, and freedom that shaped our nations' founding.

A Revolutionary Cooking Soundtrack

ABOUT THE AUTHOR

Elizabeth Winslow is an author, world traveler, and storyteller who brings both history and imagination vividly to life. With a deep passion for uncovering forgotten voices and preserving cultural memory, she writes historical fiction and nonfiction that illuminate the American Revolution in fresh and compelling ways. Drawing from authentic letters, recipes, and artifacts, her work invites readers into the kitchens, parlors, and battlefields of the eighteenth century—revealing the human stories behind history.

Her works include *Lost Letters of the American Revolution*. This nonfiction collection blends archival research with narrative storytelling, and *Lost Recipes of the American Revolution*, which pairs authentic period "receipts" with modern adaptations to help readers experience the flavors of colonial America. She is also the author of *Ashes to Liberty*, a historical romance set during the turbulent years leading up to the Revolution.

Winslow's storytelling is not confined to the past. She also writes children's literature inspired by the moral clarity of classic fables. Her works for younger readers, including *The Prince with No Name and* The Fables of Avalon — explore themes of honor, kindness, courage, and compassion, offering stories that will resonate across generations, soon to be released.

Throughout her writing, Elizabeth Winslow seeks to connect the past and the present, fact and imagination. Whether uncovering forgotten correspondence or crafting timeless tales, her work reflects a single guiding purpose: to awaken curiosity, wonder, and courage in every reader she reaches.

SOURCES

Adams, John. *The Adams Papers: Diary and Autobiography of John Adams.* Vol. 1. Cambridge: Harvard University Press, 1961.

Brewer, Priscilla. "Cider in Colonial New England." *Colonial Williamsburg Journal,* Winter 2007. https://research.colonialwilliamsburg.org/.

Carter, Susannah. *The Frugal Housewife: Or, Complete Woman Cook.* London: Edes and Gill, 1772. Facsimile via Internet Archive.

Child, Lydia Maria. *The American Frugal Housewife.* Boston: Carter and Hendee, 1832. Project Gutenberg.

Conroy, David W. *In Public Houses: Drink and the Revolution of Authority in Colonial Massachusetts.* Chapel Hill: University of North Carolina Press, 1995.

Cubbison, Douglas R. *The Battle of Saratoga, 1777: Control of the Hudson River Valley.* Albany: SUNY Press, 2014.

Draper, Mary. *Bread for Soldiers.* April 1775. Cited in "Chapter History," Mary Draper Chapter, Daughters of the American Revolution. https://marydraperdar.org/chapter-history.html.

Earle, Alice Morse. *Home Life in Colonial Days.* New York: Macmillan, 1898.

Faull, Katherine. *Moravian Women's Memoirs: Their Related Lives, 1750–1820.* Syracuse: Syracuse University Press, 1997.

Glasse, Hannah. *The Art of Cookery Made Plain and Easy.* London: Printed for the Author, 1747. Facsimile editions via Project Gutenberg and Internet Archive.

Greene, Jerome A. *The Guns of Independence: The Siege of Yorktown, 1781.* Savas Beatie, 2005.

Hess, Karen. *Martha Washington's Booke of Cookery.* New York: Columbia University Press, 1981.

Holmes, Richard. *Redcoat: The British Soldier in the Age of Horse and Musket.* New York: HarperCollins, 2002.

Ketchum, Richard M. *Saratoga: Turning Point of America's Revolutionary War*. New York: Henry Holt, 1997.

Martin, Joseph Plumb. *A Narrative of a Revolutionary Soldier*. 1830. Reprint, New York: Signet Classics, 2001.

Mount Vernon Ladies' Association. "Asparagus Soup." *Mount Vernon Inn Recipes*. Accessed September 6, 2025. https://www.mountvernon.org/inn/recipes/article/asparagus-soup.

———. "What George Washington Ate." Accessed September 2025. https://www.mountvernon.org/george-washington/facts/what-did-george-washington-eat.

National Park Service. "18th-Century Recipes from New Jersey." Accessed 2025. https://www.nps.gov/articles/000/18th-century-nj-recipes.htm.

———. "Washington-Rochambeau Revolutionary Route." Accessed 2025. https://www.nps.gov/articles/washington-rochambeau-route.htm.

Randolph, Mary. *The Virginia House-Wife; Or, Directionsical Cook*. Washington, DC: Davis and Force, 1824.

Rees, Jonathan. *Food and Drink in Colonial and Revolutionary America*. Westport, CT: Greenwood Press, 2007.

Simmons, Amelia. *American Cookery*. Hartford: Hudson and Goodwin, 1796. Reprinted at Feeding America Digital Archive. https://d.lib.msu.edu/fa/29.

Smith, Andrew F. *Eating History: Thirty Turning Points in the Making of American Cuisine*. New York: Columbia University Press, 2009.

Smith, Eliza. *The Compleat Housewife*. Williamsburg: William Parks, 1742.

Smithsonian Magazine. "Colonial Recipes: Sally Lunn Cake." https://www.smithsonianmag.com/arts-culture/colonial-recipes-sally-lunn-cake-82438919/.

Townsends. "Making Spruce Beer in the 18th Century." YouTube video, March 27, 2015. https://www.youtube.com/watch?v=x8bCqQ6xGx4.

Virginia Museum of History and Culture. "Bound to the Fire: How Virginia's Enslaved Cooks Helped Invent American Cuisine." https://virginiahistory.org/learn/bound-fire-how-virginias-enslaved-cooks-helped-invent-american-cuisine.

Wilson, David K. *The Southern Strategy: Britain's Conquest of South Carolina and Georgia, 1775–1780*. Columbia: University of South Carolina Press, 2005.

GLOSSARY OF COLONIAL TERMS

Bohea—A popular black tea imported from China in the eighteenth century. Much of the tea dumped into Boston Harbor in 1773 was Bohea.

Election Cake—A spiced fruit cake traditionally baked for Election Day festivities in New England. It combined abundance with civic ritual.

Flip—A colonial mixed drink made by plunging a red-hot poker into ale, rum, and sugar to heat and froth it. Popular in taverns and among soldiers.

Hoecake—A simple cornmeal cake baked on the flat of a hoe or griddle. Beloved by George Washington, it became a symbol of early American food.

Negus—A warm punch of wine, sugar, lemon, and spices, often served at social gatherings. Today, we would recognize it as a form of mulled wine.

Pottage—A thick stew or soup made from vegetables, grains, and sometimes meat; a sustaining dish that fed both families and soldiers.

Pye—The period spelling of *pie*. Pies could be savory (filled with meat or fowl) or sweet (filled with fruit or custard) and were staples of colonial cookery.

Receipt—The eighteenth-century term for what we now call a *recipe*. A receipt was typically brief, assuming the cook already knew the *Directions* through experience and practice.

Sack—A fortified white wine imported from Spain and used in cooking or punch bowls. Similar to modern sherry.

Sallet—The colonial word for *salad,* usually referring to a mix of herbs or lightly dressed vegetables.

Seed Cake—A lightly sweet cake flavored with caraway or other

Syllabub—A frothy dessert drink made with cream, sugar, and wine or cider, whipped until light. Commonly served at festive occasions.

Toddy—A drink of spirits, hot water, sugar, and spices—the colonial version of a hot cocktail, often taken for "medicinal" purposes.

Wassail—A spiced cider punch served at Christmas or New Year's. The name derives from the Old English toast *Waes hael*—" be healthy."

INDEX OF RECIPES

D

O

YOUR KITCHEN NOTES

Use these pages to:

- Record ingredient changes
- Note the cooking times that worked best in your kitchen
- Adapt recipes for modern tools or dietary needs
- Preserve family memories tied to these dishes

A well-used cookbook tells a story far beyond its printed pages.

Eighteenth-century cooks often kept their own handwritten notes—adjusting receipts to taste, availability, and circumstance. Margins were filled with observations, corrections, and personal touches passed from one kitchen to the next.

The following blank pages honor that tradition. You can use them to record your own adaptations, reflections, and household wisdom.

Notes

Notes

Notes

Notes

Notes

Notes

Notes

Notes

Notes

Notes

Notes

Notes

Notes

Notes

Notes

Notes

Notes

Notes

Notes

Notes

Notes

Notes

Notes

Notes

Notes

Notes

Notes

Notes

Notes

Notes

Notes

Notes

Notes

Notes

Notes

Notes

Notes